The Best Test Preparation for the

GREEN
EDITION

U.S. Postal Exams

SSF

473/473c

4th Edition

Wallie Walker-Hammond

Planet Friendly Publishing
✔ Made in the United States
✔ Printed on Recycled Paper
Learn more at www.greenedition.org

At REA we're committed to producing books in an earth-friendly manner and to helping our customers make greener choices.

Manufacturing books in the United States ensures compliance with strict environmental laws and eliminates the need for international freight shipping, a major contributor to global air pollution.

And printing on recycled paper helps minimize our consumption of trees, water and fossil fuels. **The Best Test Preparation for the U.S. Postal Exams 473/473c** was printed on paper made with **10% post-consumer waste.** According to Environmental Defense's Paper Calculator, by using this innovative paper instead of conventional papers, we achieved the following environmental benefits:

Trees Saved: 6 • Air Emissions Eliminated: 955 pounds
Water Saved: 938 gallons • Solid Waste Eliminated: 372 pounds

For more information on our environmental practices, please visit us online at **www.rea.com/green**

Research & Education Association
61 Ethel Road West
Piscataway, New Jersey 08854
E-mail: info@rea.com

The Best Test Preparation for the U.S. Postal Examinations 473/473c

Printed in the United States of America

Library of Congress Control Number 2008940694

ISBN-13: 978-0-7386-0145-8
ISBN-10: 0-7386-0145-4

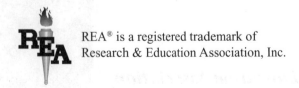

REA® is a registered trademark of Research & Education Association, Inc.

TABLE OF CONTENTS

ABOUT THE AUTHOR

Wallie Walker-Hammond is an author and editor of more than 65 test preparation titles. Her extensive experience in testing includes more than 20 years as an assessment specialist at Educational Testing Service.

ACKNOWLEDGMENTS

In addition to our author, we would like to thank Larry B. Kling, Vice President, Editorial, for his overall direction; Pam Weston, Vice President, Publishing, for setting the quality standards for production integrity and managing the publication to completion; Michael Reynolds, Managing Editor, for editorial contributions and project management; Christine Saul, Senior Graphic Artist, for designing our cover; Jeff LoBalbo, Senior Graphic Designer, for coordinating prepress electronic file mapping, and ATLIS Graphics for designing and typesetting this edition.

ABOUT REA

Founded in 1959, Research & Education Association (REA) is dedicated to publishing the finest and most effective educational materials—including software, study guides, and test preps—for students in middle school, high school, college, graduate school, and beyond.

REA's test preparation series includes books and software for all academic levels in almost all disciplines. REA publishes test preps for students who have not yet entered high school, as well as high school students preparing to enter college. Students from countries around the world seeking to attend college in the United States will find the assistance they need in REA's publications. For college students seeking advanced degrees, REA publishes test preps for many major graduate school admission examinations in a wide variety of disciplines, including engineering, law, and medicine. Students at every level, in every field, with every ambition can find what they are looking for among REA's publications.

REA's publications and educational materials are highly regarded and continually receive an unprecedented amount of praise from professionals, instructors, librarians, parents, and students. Our authors are as diverse as the subject matter represented in the books we publish. They are well known in their respective disciplines and serve on the faculties of prestigious colleges and universities throughout the United States and Canada.

We invite you to visit us at *www.rea.com* to find out how "REA is making the world smarter."

POSTAL EXAMINATION

Applying to the Postal Service

APPLYING TO THE POSTAL SERVICE 1

CONSIDERING A CAREER WITH THE POSTAL SERVICE

Founded on September 26, 1789, the Post Office Department became a permanent federal agency in 1792. Today's United States Postal Service (USPS)—transformed into an independent establishment of the executive branch in 1971—has become one of the largest and most efficient entities of any kind in the world, delivering more than 200 billion pieces of mail annually. The Postal Service employs more than 800,000 people, who process and carry more mail to more people over a larger geographic area than in any other country. Retirements and expansion have created the need for tens of thousands of new employees in recent years. The USPS offers a secure career with good pay and opportunities for advancement, which makes working for the Postal Service a wise investment in your future.

If you are interested in job security, consider that the U.S. Postal Service offers a solid array of benefits, including health and life insur-

Founded on September 26, 1789, the Post Office Department became a permanent federal agency in 1792.

ance, a retirement plan, a savings/investment plan with employer contribution, a flexible spending account, flextime scheduling of core work hours, and annual vacation and sick leave. Qualified applicants must pass a pre-employment drug screening to meet the requirement to be drug free. Applicants must also be U.S. citizens or have permanent resident alien status.

There are opportunities for advancement for all. The USPS policy directs that employee promotions be made solely on ability, without regard to race, sex, age, religion, or political-party affiliation. On-the-job training and advancement courses are also offered. New technologies typically create the sense of job elimination, but in the case of the Postal Service, the volume of mail has continued to increase. An ever-increasing population, along with the increase in direct-mail advertising that comes with an expanding economy, keeps the need for postal workers high. If you think that the use of e-mail could threaten the postal business, remember that the Postal Service is itself a major e-mail service provider. The United States Postal Service reaches every person, every day. In fact, after more than 200 years, the Postal Service is as dedicated as ever to providing quality service to all of its customers.

Description of Positions

An employee of the Postal Service has the opportunity to transfer to other locations or bid for other positions. It is important to keep on top of advancements in the various positions. Because you will be making a career choice to enter the Postal Service, a lot of thought may be necessary when choosing the position for which you will be applying. Included here are brief descriptions of the major positions for which you may apply. It is a good idea to speak with a representative from the USPS before you choose this career path. Speak with family or friends employed by the USPS, your local carrier, the postmaster at your local office, or even a window clerk if you can.

It is important to keep on top of advancements in the various positions.

Carrier
Requirements: Test 473

The job of postal carrier may be the most recognized position in the Postal Service. Postal carriers find their jobs extremely rewarding, citing the relationship that they develop with their communities as one of the major pluses of the job. There are also many behind-the-scenes requirements of a mail carrier.

Carriers typically arrive early for their jobs, between 6 A.M. and 8 A.M. The mail must be sorted, racked, and tied before it can be loaded. Carriers deliver and collect mail on foot or by vehicle. Carriers may be required to carry mailbags on their shoulders. A mailbag full of mail can weigh up to 35 pounds and carriers will be required to load and unload trays and containers of mail and parcels up to 70 pounds. City carrier applicants must have a valid state driver's license. Carriers must also check on changes of address, undeliverable mail, and special deliveries such as cash on delivery (COD) that involve customers on their route. If you work as a rural carrier, you may sell stamps, carrier scales, and other mailing equipment, and take other services to those customers who cannot visit a town office.

The advantages of this job are many. Carriers can work at his or her own pace as long as the mail is delivered by a specific time. A relationship can be built between the carrier and the community. Carriers can aid lost pedestrians, especially children. If you like exercise in the outdoors, this position may be right for you. Expect a lot of exposure to the outdoors, in both good and bad weather.

The job of postal carrier may be the most recognized position in the Postal Service.

Distribution Clerk
Requirements: Test 473

Distribution clerks may work either at the front window or in the distribution center. Letters must be grouped into categories: letters, parcel post, and magazines and newspapers. The letters are either fed into stamp-canceling machines or are canceled by hand. Then they are taken to be sorted by destination: local area, nearby state, groups of distant states, or large individual cities. For instance, mail to New York or Chicago is sorted into its own bin. If an automatic machine is being used, the clerk must enter codes that instruct the machine to send the mail to the correct bin. Larger postal centers may have clerks working around the clock. Night workers usually receive a higher salary. A distribution clerk must have good eyesight. A candidate for this position will need to attain a good reading score on the eye exam to be considered. Corrective lenses are permitted.

Window clerks are responsible for helping customers who visit the post office. They may sell stamps, write money orders, register mail,

A candidate for distribution clerk will need to attain a good reading score on the eye exam to be considered.

weigh packages for correct postage, or check packages to make sure they are sturdy enough to be mailed.

Flat Sorting Machine Operator
Requirements: Test 473

Flat sorting machine operators must be able to handle a physically demanding job. They are responsible for handling large packages. They will be trained on automated machines to sort packages.

Mark-Up Clerk
Requirements: Test 473

A person in this position will be utilizing a computerized forwarding system (CFS), which is among the newest technology on the scene. The clerk must use the computer to generate a database of the customers who have recently changed their addresses and use the machine to make labels for the mail being rerouted for these customers.

Mail Handler
Requirements: Test 473

Mail handlers have one of the most physically demanding jobs in the Postal Service. They are required to lift heavy items, up to 70 pounds. Work is done mainly in the dock area, loading and unloading mail. They may also work in the mail-canceling section, moving mail from one location to another. Mail handlers are trained on many pieces of equipment: forklifts, rewrapping machines, addressographs, and mimeographs. A physical test—consisting of being able to carry two 70-pound bags to a truck, moving it to another area, unloading the truck, then returning it to its original position—is required.

Mail handlers are required to lift heavy items, up to 70 pounds.

Mail Processor
Requirements: Test 473

Mail processors use a special automated machine called an optical character reader (OCR). This machine reads the bar codes found on many labeled pieces of mail. Mail processors also collate, bundle, and load the mail into the appropriate bins. Because mail processors have knowledge of the computerized equipment, they may help to trouble-shoot the equipment.

Rural Carrier Associate
Requirements: Test 460

Rural carrier associates are noncareer USPS employees. They either serve as a leave replacement in the absence of a regular rural carrier or provide extra service like selling stamps and other mailing equipment on auxiliary routes. After one year of service, an associate has bidding rights to USPS career vacancies as they occur.

Applying

Are You Eligible?
Before you begin the work necessary to apply to take the postal exam, you should read the following list. If you can answer yes to all of the questions, then you are eligible to take the test. If you answer no to a question, you should speak with a postal service representative before investing your time and effort.

- Are you a high school graduate or are you certified through local authorities to have terminated formal education for a valid reason?

- Will you be eighteen years of age at the time of employment (not necessarily when you take the exam)?

- Are you a U.S. citizen or do you hold permanent resident alien status?

- Can you pass a routine physical, including tests for hearing and sight and a urinalysis test that screens for illegal substances?

When to Apply
This may be the trickiest part of obtaining a Postal Service career. On average, the 473 Battery Test is given only once every three years by any postal center. Some larger postal centers give the test more frequently. The 460 Rural Carrier Associates Exam is given at least once a year. Some districts offer it several times a year, depending on the need for

Exam Fact

You must be active in your search for registration periods.

new employees. The tests are not given at the same time in every office, so you will have to do some research. First, you need to identify the area to which you would like to apply. You can do this by receiving information on office locations through your local post office. On the application, you will be asked to choose three specific post offices. You need to find out when the next set of tests will be given for the area on which you have chosen to concentrate. It will be necessary to call the personnel office or visit the postal bulletin board to check for registration announcements. You may also subscribe to a listing of government jobs, which will list registration dates. Some offices may post announcements over public service stations. You must be active in your search for registration periods. It is not unlikely that the office will accept registration for only one week. If you would consider commuting to a more distant location, you may find a test in another area that will be given sooner than the one in your area of initial interest. It is possible to transfer once you have established yourself in your job.

Exam Fact

You may take the 473 exam more than once.

Some postal districts offer a different type of registration and testing system. Open Testing Exam System (OPTEX) uses a longer application period, so you may have an easier time applying in one of these districts. In this system, your name is put into a computer that randomly draws names of applicants to sit for the exam as the need to hire arises. On the positive side, this system usually offers exams more frequently than the traditional testing pattern. However, you may spend some time waiting for your name to be drawn randomly from the list of applicants. It is a chance that some people take because they hope to be one of the lucky ones who have their name drawn early.

You may take this exam more than once. If you are taking the exam for the same position, however, you may not take the same version of the test that you took previously. You will need to wait until the Postal Service changes editions. Taking as many tests for as many positions as possible will benefit you by keeping your name ready to be called.

How to Fill Out an Application

Once you learn that they are accepting applications, go to *www.usps.com/employment* and apply online. The application will have two parts for you to fill in. It is important to complete both sections carefully and accurately. Any application not completed correctly will be discarded. Keep the two sections together. Separated applications will also be discarded. The

Exam Fact

Keep the two sections together.

reverse side of the application contains the directions necessary to complete the application. Complete the application as quickly as possible and return it to the personnel department yourself so that you will not worry about whether it will make it there in time for the deadline.

Once your application has been processed, you will receive half of the application form in the mail. It is very important to keep this form because it will serve as your ticket into the testing room. Along with your application card, you will receive information about where and when the exam will take place. Write this information down in a place you will not forget.

A sample answer sheet will accompany your registration card. It is important to fill this sheet out completely. Some of the questions require information that may slip your mind come test day. Take this sheet with you to the test center. It will aid you in filling out the official answer sheet the day of the test.

Sample questions will also be sent to you. It is a good idea to complete these questions as you would the questions in this book. A little extra practice can't hurt. Look it over so you know what to expect.

A little extra practice can't hurt.

THE DAY OF THE EXAM

Practicing for the postal exam should begin well in advance of the actual exam. Cramming the night before will not benefit you. In fact, it may serve to create stress, which can detract from your score. The night before the exam should be spent in a calm, relaxed fashion. Get plenty of sleep! Be sure to eat a good breakfast so a growling stomach will not cause anxiety or distraction.

When you arrive at the testing center (preferably with time to spare), be sure to have your admission card, sample answer sheet, a picture form of identification—such as a driver's license—and two #2 pencils. Consider dressing lightly; you may wish to carry a sweater or jacket, which can be doffed or donned to adjust for the temperature in the room. Whatever you wear, be sure it is comfortable. Leave your house early to allow time for any problems on the road. Latecomers will not be admitted to the test center.

Latecomers will not be admitted to the test center.

Once you are seated in the exam room, you will be given an official answer sheet; copy the information that you put on your sample answer sheet onto this official answer sheet. It is important to have your sample sheet with you because you will be given only fifteen minutes to transfer the information. You will be asked to choose three specific locations in which you would like employment. Therefore, it is necessary to have researched this thoroughly beforehand. You will also be asked to specify the positions for which you are applying. Again, you must conduct research to find the best position suited to your abilities.

The examiner, along with the monitors, will hand out the testing packet. Specific directions are given concerning when to complete certain steps in the testing process. Examiners are very strict on examinee compliance with these directions. You will have your test invalidated if you fail to follow the directions, so listen carefully.

FORMAT OF POSTAL EXAM 473

The 473 exam has four sections. Each section tests skills that the Postal Service requires of its employees. These qualities include a good memory, quick decision-making ability, and the ability to follow directions. The Postal Service prides itself on being able to deliver its mail quickly and accurately. Included in this section is a brief description of each part of the test, along with a few sample questions.

The Postal Service prides itself on being able to deliver its mail quickly and accurately.

Part A: Address Checking

In this section, you are asked to compare two lists of addresses, deciding if they are alike or different. If the addresses are alike, darken oval "A," for "No Errors"; if the difference reflects a difference in the address only, darken oval "B"; if the difference is in the ZIP code only, darken oval "C"; if the difference is in both the address and the ZIP code, darken oval "D." This section focuses on speed and accuracy. You will be given eleven minutes to compare sixty addresses. While you are not expected to complete this entire section, the object is to combine a fast enough pace with enough accuracy to get a high score. Here is an example of Part A.

A. No Errors	B. Address Only	C. ZIP Code Only	D. Both

Correct List

	Address	ZIP Code
1.	590 Bridge St. Macon, GA	31201
2.	3903 Hellington Ave. Trenton, NJ	08618
3.	21 Central Ave. W. Minneapolis, MN	55401
4.	123 4th Street Franklin, NJ	08873
5.	8639 Elsie Rd., Apt. 3 Lawrenceville, TX	79111

List to Be Checked

	Address	ZIP Code
1.	590 Bridje St. Macon, GA	31210
2.	3093 Hellington Ave. Trenton, NJ	08618
3.	21 Central Ave. W. Minneapolis, MN	55401
4.	1234 4th Street Franklin, NJ	08837
5.	8639 Elsie Rd., Apt. 3 Lawrenceville, TX	79911

Answer Grid				
1.	Ⓐ	Ⓑ	Ⓒ	●
2	Ⓐ	●	Ⓒ	Ⓓ
3.	●	Ⓑ	Ⓒ	Ⓓ
4.	Ⓐ	Ⓑ	Ⓒ	●
5.	Ⓐ	Ⓑ	●	Ⓓ

Part B: Forms Completion

In this section, you will be tested on your ability to identify information needed to complete forms that are similar to forms used by the Postal Service. Part B of the test consists of thirty questions to be completed in fifteen minutes. Answer each question based on the information provided in the forms. Here is an example of Part B.

INSURED MAIL RECEIPT	
OFFICIAL USE	
1. Postage $	**4.** Special Handling Fee
2. **2a.** ☐ Fragile **2b.** ☐ Perishable **2c.** ☐ Liquid **2d.** ☐ Hazardous	**5.** Total Postage & Fees $
3. Insurance Fee: **3a.** Insurance Coverage:	**6.** Postmark Here
7. *Sent to:*	
8. *Street, Apt. No., or PO Box No.*	
9. *City, State, ZIP+4*	

1. Where would you check that the item is perishable?

    A. Box 1

    B. Box 2a

    C. Box 2b

    D. Box 3

2. Which of the following would be a correct entry for Box 6?

    A. A check mark

    B. Post office stamp

    C. $2.35

    D. Kathy Smith

3. Where should the post office box number be entered on this form?

    A. Box 1

    B. Box 6

    C. Box 7

    D. Box 8

4. Which of these is a correct entry for Box 3a?

 A. Yes

 B. $5.67

 C. Randy Zisk

 D. 76543

5. Which of these is a correct entry for Box 9?

 A. 2486 Center Street

 B. 2486 Center St., Trenton

 C. 2486 Center St., Trenton, NJ

 D. Trenton, NJ 08618-1919

Answer Grid				
1.	Ⓐ	Ⓑ	⬤	D
2	Ⓐ	⬤	Ⓒ	Ⓓ
3.	Ⓐ	Ⓑ	Ⓒ	⬤
4.	⬤	Ⓑ	Ⓒ	Ⓓ
5.	Ⓐ	Ⓑ	Ⓒ	⬤

Part C: Section 1: Coding

Part C consists of two sections, Coding and Memory. The Coding section has thirty-six questions to be completed in six minutes. The Memory section has thirty-six questions to be completed in seven minutes. In this part of the test, you must demonstrate how well you can use codes quickly and accurately. A coding guide will be presented for Section 1, and you must use your memorization skills to remember the coding guide for Section 2. As best as you can, you must find the correct code for each address given. In Section 2, you must assign a code to the address given based on the same coding guide that you used previously and memorized. Remember that while you are working with the coding guide in Section 1, you will need to remember that same guide. Try to memorize the guide as you use it in Section 1; you will need to know it for Section 2.

Here is an example of Section 1.

Directions: Assign a code to questions 1–36 based on the coding guide below.

<table>
<tr><td colspan="2" align="center">CODING GUIDE</td></tr>
<tr><td align="center">Address Range</td><td align="center">Delivery Route</td></tr>
<tr><td align="center">1–99 E. State St.
50–599 N. Broad St.
1–299 N. Temple Rd.</td><td align="center">A</td></tr>
<tr><td align="center">100–299 E. State St.
300–600 N. Temple Rd.</td><td align="center">B</td></tr>
<tr><td align="center">600–800 N. Broad St.
20–100 Center St.
1500–4500 N. Main St.</td><td align="center">C</td></tr>
<tr><td align="center">All mail that doesn't fall in one of the address ranges listed above</td><td align="center">D</td></tr>
</table>

	Address	Delivery Route			
1.	39 E. State Street	A	B	C	D
2.	35 Center St.	A	B	C	D
3.	400 Temple Rd.	A	B	C	D
4.	255 E. State Street	A	B	C	D
5.	100 Center St.	A	B	C	D
6.	2501 S. Main St.	A	B	C	D
7.	2505 N. Main St.	A	B	C	D
8.	199 N. Temple Rd.	A	B	C	D
9.	598-A N. Broad St.	A	B	C	D
10.	600 Center St.	A	B	C	D

Answer Grid				
1.	●	B	C	D
2	A	B	●	D
3.	A	B	C	●
4.	A	●	C	D
5.	A	B	●	D
6.	A	B	C	●
7.	A	B	●	D
8.	●	B	C	D
9.	●	B	C	D
10.	A	B	C	●

Part C: Section 2: Memory

In Section 2 of the test, you will assign codes based on your memory of the coding guide from Section 1. During Section 1, you are allowed to look at the coding guide, but during Section 2, you have to assign codes based on your memory of the same coding guide. Here is an example of Section 2.

Directions: Take three minutes to memorize the coding guide below. Assign a code based on your memory of the coding guide. This coding guide is the same guide used in the previous coding section.

CODING GUIDE	
Address Range	**Delivery Route**
1–99 E. State St. 50–599 N. Broad St. 1–299 N. Temple Rd.	A
100–299 E. State St. 300–600 N. Temple Rd.	B
600–800 N. Broad St. 20–100 Center St. 1500–4500 N. Main St.	C
All mail that doesn't fall in one of the address ranges listed above	D

	Address	Delivery Route			
1.	53 E. State St.	A	B	C	D
2.	199 N. Temple Rd.	A	B	C	D
3.	599 S. Broad St.	A	B	C	D
4.	20 Center St., Apt. 5	A	B	C	D
5.	143 E. State St.	A	B	C	D
6.	4000 N. Temple Rd.	A	B	C	D
7.	4400 N. Main St.	A	B	C	D
8.	500 N. Main St.	A	B	C	D
9.	50 N. Broad St.	A	B	C	D
10.	319 N. Temple Rd.	A	B	C	D

Answer Grid				
1.	●	Ⓑ	Ⓒ	Ⓓ
2	●	Ⓑ	Ⓒ	Ⓓ
3.	Ⓐ	Ⓑ	Ⓒ	●
4.	Ⓐ	Ⓑ	●	Ⓓ
5.	Ⓐ	●	Ⓒ	Ⓓ
6.	Ⓐ	Ⓑ	Ⓒ	●
7.	Ⓐ	Ⓑ	●	Ⓓ
8.	Ⓐ	Ⓑ	Ⓒ	●
9.	●	Ⓑ	Ⓒ	Ⓓ
10.	Ⓐ	●	Ⓒ	Ⓓ

AFTER THE TEST

When the test is completed, your answer sheet will be sent to a center where a machine will grade your test paper automatically. This is why filling in the ovals correctly is crucial. After the paper is scored, you will be given a score. The formula for this scoring is not available to the public. As you proceed through this book, however, you will be scoring your tests, coming up with a raw score. The Postal Service finds your raw score in this same fashion, then adjusts it with the confidential formula. Allow four to eight weeks to receive your scores. The passing score is 70. If your score is below 70, you will receive a notice stating that your score was not high enough to pass. You will need to try the test again at a later date if you wish to continue the process. If you achieve a passing score, you will receive your score along with the location to which your name will be sent.

Exam Fact

Filling in the ovals correctly is crucial.

Once your scores have been sent to the location you specify, you are put on what is called a register of eligibles. This list contains names of those people who are eligible for employment by the Postal Service. Where your name is placed on the list depends on your score. The higher your score, the higher your name will appear on the list. As positions become available and people are called for employment, names are removed from the list. When your name is chosen from the top of the list, you will receive an application for employment. This application must be completed and returned to the post office where you are being hired. You will be notified of dates and times for an interview and physical.

Names remain on the register of eligibles for a period of two years. If your name does not come up for employment after two years, you may extend your eligibility for another year. Three years is the maximum time a name can spend on a register of eligibles. If you wish to have your eligibility extended an extra year, you must put your request in writing to the postmaster between the eighteenth and twenty-fourth month. It is important to remember to put this request in writing. Once two years have elapsed, your name will be stricken from the register unless you notify the post office otherwise.

Three years is the maximum time a name can spend on a register of eligibles.

The last item concerning scoring is the five- to ten-point preference given to veterans. If a veteran meets certain requirements for serving his or her country, it is assumed he or she should receive preferential treatment. His or her name will be placed five to ten points higher than his or her original score if it is above the 70-point passing mark. This person is placed before all others who receive that same grade. Here is a list of requirements for receiving the veteran's benefit. If you feel you may be eligible for this benefit, you must complete the section on the official answer sheet concerning veterans. You will be asked for proof of this veteran status.

Five extra points are awarded if the applicant served in active duty

- during a war
  - ▶ between April 28, 1952, and July 1, 1955
  - ▶ on any campaign or expedition during which a campaign badge was authorized
  - ▶ for more than 180 consecutive days, any part of which occurred after January 31, 1955, and before October 15, 1976

▶ in Southeast Asia on or after August 2, 1990, and if awarded a Southeast Asia Service Medal

Ten points are added if:

- you were disabled while on active duty or awarded a Purple Heart

- you are a wife of a disabled veteran and if the veteran is physically disqualified due to service-connected disabilities to return to his usual occupation

- you are a widow of a serviceman who died on active duty (only if not remarried)

- you are the mother of a deceased or disabled veteran son or daughter

- you are widowed, divorced, or separated, or your present husband is permanently and totally disabled

Assessing Your Skills

CHAPTER

2

ASSESSING YOUR SKILLS

2

SUGGESTIONS FOR TAKING THE DIAGNOSTIC TEST

You should use this chapter to gauge your ability to take the postal exam as prepared as you are right now. It is important to know your likely score on this exam before you begin studying. By doing this, you will be able to chart your progress, and if you follow this guide carefully, you will make progress. Your first lesson deals with completing the diagnostic test answer sheet correctly.

In Chapter 1, you were introduced to the four question types. All of the question types require you to fill in an oval on your answer sheet. There are actually correct and incorrect ways to fill in an oval. The trick is learning to fill the oval in as quickly as possible. Remember, time is a key factor for this test. You do not want to wastc time filling in ovals.

Begin all of the exams with properly prepared pencils. You must bring two #2 pencils into the exam room. Prepare your pencil points a day or two before the exam. You can prepare your pencil points in one of

Exam Fact

Remember, time is a key factor for this test.

23

two ways. The points should not be pinpoint sharp; a dull point is good. This will give you more lead surface on the paper, which means that it will take less movement of the pencil to fill in the oval. Work your pencil point to a dull slant. You may also chisel a 45-degree slant on your pencil point. Work at perfecting this point. The time spent doing this will pay off in the long run. Remember to prepare two pencils with the slanted point.

Because a machine reads your answer sheet, it is important to answer the questions in a manner the machine can read. The oval you choose should be filled in as completely as possible, with no lead going over the edge. The machine may understand stray marks as two filled-in ovals. This will result in a wrong answer because only one answer is allowed per line. The following are incorrectly completed answers and a correctly completed answer. Be sure your ovals look like the correct choice.

Incorrect

Correct

Once you understand the correct way to complete your answer choice, you need to perfect filling in the ovals to maximize your time. Because your pencil has a slanted 45-degree angle point, you will be able to cover the oval with a lead mark in one or two swipes of the pencil on the paper. Your arm and hand should not be moving. Small, precise movements by the fingers save you time and energy. Covering the oval in one swipe may not be easy at first. You must remember to cover it completely enough so the computer can read it. Therefore, practice sheets have been provided for you. For the exam, you will use an answer sheet that contains four ovals. The objective here is to become comfortable filling in the blanks with one or two quick swipes of your pencil. This exercise should be taken very seriously. You can save time by speeding up your filling-in technique.

Exam Fact

You can save time by speeding up your filling-in technique.

Now you are ready to take the diagnostic test. The directions for each section have been provided for you as part of the exam. Focus on this diagnostic exam as you would on the actual test so you can get a true reading of your strengths and of areas in which you need improvement. Sit at a table where there is ample lighting. Be sure there are no distracting noises and no possibility of interruption before you have finished the entire preliminary exam. After you have finished the exam, check your answers with the correct answers following the test. Mark your scores on the chart provided. An explanation of the chart follows the exam. Remember to fill in the answer blanks correctly. When you have your testing location and atmosphere set and your #2 pencils prepared correctly, you can begin the diagnostic exam.

Do not panic if you find this test difficult or confusing. After completing this book, you will feel confident in your ability to pass the real exam with a high score. Chapter 3 includes techniques to help you prepare.

Diagnostic Test

PART A—ADDRESS CHECKING

11 Minutes
60 Questions

Directions: In this section, compare the List to Be Checked with the Correct List. Decide if there are No Errors (A), an error in the Address Only (B), an error in the ZIP Code Only (C), or an error in Both the Address and the ZIP Code.

A. No Errors	B. Address Only	C. ZIP Code Only	D. Both

	Correct List		List to Be Checked	
	Address	ZIP Code	Address	ZIP Code
1.	372 Hickory Drive Charlotte, NC	26227	374 Hickory Street Charlotte, NC	27227
2.	38 Howard Street Indianapolis, IN	46254	38 Howard Street Indianapolis, IN	46254
3.	2112 First St. Apt. 3D Philadelphia, PA	19131	2112 First St. Apt. 3 Philadelphia, PA	19131
4.	2009 Interstate 9 Naperville, IL	60565	2009 Interstate 9 Naperville, IL	60565
5.	500 Sunnydale Drive Washington, DC	20018	5000 Sunnydale Drive Washington, DC	20018
6.	99 Thistle Lake Hyattsville, MD	21217	99 Thistle Lake Hyattsville, MD	21217

A. No Errors	B. Address Only	C. ZIP Code Only	D. Both

	Correct List			List to Be Checked	
	Address	*ZIP Code*		*Address*	*ZIP Code*
7.	48B First Ave NW Neptune, NJ	07753		48B First Ave N Neptune, NJ	07753
8.	75 Route 516 Nottoway, VA	23955		75 Route 516 Nottoway, VA	23955
9.	8001 Hwy. No. 29 El Paso, TX	79924		9001 Hwy. No. 29 El Paso, TX	79924
10.	8 Winding Lake Drive Listonia, GA	30038		8 Winding Lake Rd Listonia, GA	30338
11.	3 Houston Drive Woodside, NY	11377		3 Horston Drive Woodside, NY	11377
12.	48 Calada Way Detroit, MI	48204		48 Kalada Way Detroit, MI	48204
13.	38 Lenape Drive Philadelphia, PA	19104		38 Lenape Drive Philadelphia, PA	19140
14.	17 South Flatbush Road Brooklyn, NY	11213		17 South Flatbush Road Brooklyn, NY	11213
15.	205 Washington Avenue Sacramento, CA	95841		205 Washington Avenue Sacramento, CA	95841
16.	66 Homestead Lane St. John, VI	00831		66 Homestead Ct. St. John, VI	00831
17.	145 Sullivan Street Jacksonville, FL	32218		143 Sullivan Street Jacksonville, FL	32218
18.	44-B Marting Ct. Norwalk, CT	06854		44-D Marting Ct. Norwalk, CT	068545

A. No Errors	B. Address Only	C. ZIP Code Only	D. Both

	Correct List			List to Be Checked	
	Address	ZIP Code		Address	ZIP Code
19.	1014 Lakefront Terr. Wilmington, DE	19850		1014 Lakefront Ave. Wilmington, DE	19850
20.	5 Dartmouth Ave. Apt. 3B Atlanta, GA	30349		5 Dartmouth Ave. Apt. 3B Atlanta, GA	30349
21.	76 Apple Farm Road Minneapolis, MN	55417		76 Apple Farm Drive Minneapolis, MN	55417
22.	99 Senior Street Apt. 1 Chicago, IL	60620		99 Senior Street Apt. 1A Chicago, IL	60620
23.	35 Division Street Silver Spring, MD	20910		35 Dividing Street Silver Spring, MD	20910
24.	89 S. Altamonte Dr. Miami, FL	33132		89 S. Altamonte Ave Miami, FL	33132
25.	77 Rock Lake Cheyenne, WY	82007		77-C Rock Lake Cheyenne, WY	82007
26.	78 (E) Third Apt. 3B New York, NY	11216		77 (E) Third Apt. 3B New York, NY	11216
27.	90021 Denver Court Landis, NC	28088		90021 Denver Court Landis, NC	28088
28.	716 Lloyd Dr. Orange, NJ	07018		766 Lloyd Dr. Orange, NJ	07018
29.	2 Sand Hill Road Norristown, PA	19404		20 Sand Hill Road Norristown, PA	19404
30.	9 Westfield Road Charleston, SC	29403		9 Westfield Road Charleston, SC	29403

| A. No Errors | B. Address Only | C. ZIP Code Only | D. Both |

	Correct List			List to Be Checked	
	Address	*ZIP Code*		*Address*	*ZIP Code*
31.	80 Elkridge Way West Antioch, CA	94509		80 Elkridge Way West Antioch, CA	94509
32.	1776 Steward St. Staten Island, NY	10303		1776 Steward St. Staten Island, NY	10303
33.	71 Quailbrook Ct. Milwaukee, WI	53202		71 Quailbrook Ct. Milwaukee, WI	53202
34.	66 Bethany Rd. West Frederick, MD	21701		66 Bethany Rd. Frederick, MD	21701
35.	2121 Holyhock Ave. Cincinnati, OH	45242		2112 Holyhock Ave. Cincinnati, OH	45242
36.	989-C N. Falling Hill Houston, TX	77004		989-C N. Falling Hill Houston, TX	77004
37.	55 Prior Terr. Adelphi, MD	20783		55 Prior Terr. Adelphi, MD	20783
38.	86 Woodside Rd. Olympia, WA	98516		86 Wood Side Rd. Olympia, WA	95816
39.	40 Gogol Way Pine Hill, NJ	08021		40 Gogel Way Pine Hill, NJ	08021
40.	5-H Sycamore Lane Greensboro, NC	26406		5-I Sycamore Lane Greensboro, NC	26406
41.	619 Highway 51 Germantown, PA	19144		619 Highway 51 Germantown, PA	19144
42.	520 Hudson St. W. Florence, SC	29506		520 Hudson St. W. Florence, SC	29506

| A. No Errors | B. Address Only | C. ZIP Code Only | D. Both |

Correct List

	Address	ZIP Code
43.	37 Route 47 South Jacksonville, FL	32218
44.	20129 South Brush Los Angeles, CA	90043
45.	820 Winding Brook Way Durham, NC	27707
46.	318 W. 14th St. Newark, NJ	07103
47.	5 Jorgenson Lane Harrisburg, PA	17111
48.	69 Johnson Way Rochester, NY	14611
49.	10 189th St. W. Bridgeport, CT	06607
50.	52 (E) 96 Street Richmond, VA	23222
51.	5 Route 6115 Annapolis, MD	21403
52.	First & Willow Miami, FL	33127
53.	91/2 Danbury Danville, VA	24251
54.	99 Max Avenue Indianapolis, IN	46222

List to Be Checked

Address	ZIP Code
37 Route 47 North Jacksonville, FL	32218
20130 South Brush Los Angeles, CA	90043
820 Windy Brook Way Durham, NC	27707
318 W. 14th St. Newark, NJ	07103
5 Jorgenson Lane Harrisburg, PA	11111
69 Johnson Way Rochester, NY	14611
10 18th St. W. Bridgeport, CT	06607
52 W. 96 Street Richmond, VA	23222
5 Route 5116 Annapolis, MD	21403
First & Willow Miami, FL	33127
91 Danbury Danville, VA	24251
99 Max Avenue Indianapolis, IN	46222

	A. No Errors	B. Address Only	C. ZIP Code Only	D. Both

Correct List

	Address	ZIP Code
55.	36 Maya Ct. Chesapeake, VA	23325
56.	87 Thirteenth St. Memphis, TN	38117
57.	7 Vinton Circle Tampa, FL	33601
58.	40 LaGrande Avenue Brooklyn, NY	11213
59.	6889 South Ave. Wilmington, DE	19850
60.	92 Manatou Way Pittsburgh, PA	15217

List to Be Checked

Address	ZIP Code
36 Mayan Ct. Chesapeake, VA	25325
87 Thirtieth St. Memphis, TN	38117
7 Vinton Circle Tampa, FL	33610
40 LaGrande Avenue Brooklyn, NY	11213
6898 South Ave. Wilmington, DE	19850
92 Manatee Way Pittsburgh, PA	15217

PART B—FORMS COMPLETION

15 Minutes
30 Questions

Directions: Read each form and answer the questions based on the information provided.

Questions 1–7 are based on the following information.

SORRY WE MISSED YOU! WE REDELIVER FOR YOU		
1. Today's Date	**2.** Sender's Name	

3. Item is at: ___ Post Office *(see back)* _____	Available for Pick-up After **4.** Date: **5.** Time:		We will redeliver or you or your agent can pick up. See reverse.

6a. ____ Letter **6b.** ____ Large envelope, magazine, catalog, etc. **6c.** ____ Parcel **6d.** ____ Restricted Delivery **6e.** ____ Perishable Item **6f.** ____ Other:	**For Delivery:** *(Enter total number of items delivered by service type)* **For Notice Left:** *(Check applicable item)* **7a.** ____ Express Mail *(We will attempt to deliver on the next delivery day unless you instruct the post office to hold it.)* **7b.** ____ Certified **7c.** ____ Recorded Delivery **7d.** ____ Firm Bill **7e.** ____ Registered **7f.** ____ Insured **7g.** ____ Return Receipt for Merchandise **7h.** ____ Delivery Confirmation **7i.** ____ Signature Confirmation

8. ☐ If checked, you or your agent must be present at time of delivery to sign for item

9. Article Number(s)

_____

_____

_____

10. Article Requiring Payment **10a.** ☐ Postage Due **10b.** ☐ COD **10c.** ☐ Customs	**11.** Amount Due $

12. Customer Name and Address

13. ☐ **Final Notice:** Article will be returned to sender on	**14.** Delivered By and Date

1. Which of these could be a correct entry for Box 5?
   (A) 6/2/08
   (B) $11.00
   (C) 2:36 p.m.
   (D) Joe Johns

2. The notice requires a signature confirmation. Where would this be checked?
   (A) Box 6a
   (B) Box 6e
   (C) Box 7b
   (D) Box 7i

3. Where on the form would you indicate that the item is at the post office?
   (A) Box 3
   (B) Box 8
   (C) Box 12
   (D) Box 13

4. What does a check in Box 8 indicate?
   (A) The item is certified.
   (B) The item was delivered again.
   (C) The item will not be delivered without someone present.
   (D) The item will be returned to the sender.

5. The postage due is $3.75; where would this amount be entered?
   (A) Box 10a
   (B) Box 11
   (C) Box 12
   (D) Box 14

6. All of the boxes below require dates entered EXCEPT
   (A) Box 1.
   (B) Box 4.
   (C) Box 9.
   (D) Box 14.

7. Which of these could be a correct entry for Box 13?

   (A) A checkmark

   (B) 456789

   (C) Michael Reynolds

   (D) Yes

Questions 8–12 are based on the following information.

REGISTERED MAIL RECEIPT	
1. Registered No.	**8.** Date Stamp

To Be Completed By Post Office	
2. Reg. Fee	**5.** Postage
3. Handling Charge	**6.** Restricted Delivery
4. Return Receipt	**7.** Received by
9. Customer Must Declare Full Value $	Domestic Insurance up to $25,000 is included based upon the declared value. International Indemnity is limited. (See Reverse).

OFFICIAL USE
To Be Completed by Customer (Please Print) All Entries Must Be In Ballpoint or Typed
10. FROM
11. TO

8. What would be a correct entry for Box 7?

    (A) Philadelphia, PA

    (B) Peter Cooper

    (C) $250.00

    (D) 10954

9. What would be a correct entry for Box 11?

    (A) James White, 321 Carnegie Dr., Princeton, NJ 08540

    (B) (609) 123-4567

    (C) A check mark

    (D) July 15, 2008

10. Where would the date be stamped?

    (A) Box 1

    (B) Box 3

    (C) Box 8

    (D) Box 9

11. Where would a handling charge of $6.45 be entered?

    (A) Box 2

    (B) Box 3

    (C) Box 5

    (D) Box 9

12. You would enter information in all of the following boxes EXCEPT

    (A) Box 1.

    (B) Box 7.

    (C) Box 9.

    (D) Box 11.

Questions 13–19 are based on the following information.

EMPLOYEE GENERATED CHANGE OF ADDRESS	
Please PRINT items 1–7 in blue or black ink. Your initials must be entered in item 5.	
1. Change of Address for: **1a.** Individual **1b.** Entire Family Business	**2.** Start Date *(Ex. 11/14/03)* M M D D Y Y
3a. Enter LAST or Business Name **3b.** Enter FIRST Name & Middle Initial	
PRINT **OLD** mailing address below *(Number and Street Name - Include ST, AVE, CT, etc. or PO BOX number)*	
4a. OLD Mailing Address **4b.** OLD Apt. or **4c.** For Puerto Rico Only: Print urbanization Suite No. name, if appropriate. **4d.** OLD City **4e.** State **4f.** ZIP Name	
MLNA (Moved, Left No Address)	Box Closed (No Order)
5. Employee Initials	**6.** Date	**7.** Route ID Number

13. The change of address for a business should be checked in which box?

    (A) Box 1a

    (B) Box 1b

    (C) Box 1c

    (D) Box 2

14. Which of these could be an acceptable entry for Box 3a?
    (A) Jean Black
    (B) Jean A. Black
    (C) Black
    (D) Jean A.

15. Where would you indicate your initials?
    (A) Box 3b
    (B) Box 4d
    (C) Box 4e
    (D) Box 5

16. The customer has moved from Puerto Rico. Where would you enter the urbanization name?
    (A) Box 4a
    (B) Box 4c
    (C) Box 4d
    (D) Box 4e

17. Which would be a correct entry for Box 2?
    (A) 08/21/08
    (B) 8/21/08
    (C) 08/21/2008
    (D) 8/21/8

18. Where should the old ZIP code be entered?
    (A) Box 4a
    (B) Box 4b
    (C) Box 4e
    (D) Box 4f

19. What would be a correct entry for Box 4d?
    (A) Taos
    (B) New Mexico
    (C) 45 Holiday Ln.
    (D) Box 2567

Questions 20–25 are based on the following information.

COD
DELIVERY EMPLOYEE Remove Copies 1 & 2 at Time of Delivery

Collect the amount shown below, if customer pays by CHECK made payable to the mailer. **1.** Check Amount $	Collect the amount shown below if customer pays in **CASH** *(includes MO fee or fees)*. **2.** Cash Amount $

3a. ☐ Registered Mail	**3b.** ☐ Express Mail® Service	**3c.** ☐ Form 3849-D Requested

4. Date of Mailing	**5.** ☐ Remit COD Charges to Sender via Express Mail	**6.** EMCA No.

7. From:		**8.** To:

9. Delivered By	**10.** Date Delivered	**11.** Check Number
12. Date Payment Sent to Mailer	**13.** Date Form 3849-D Sent	**14.** MO Number(s)

1. DO NOT allow the recipient *(addressee or agent)* to examine the contents before payment.

2. DO NOT deliver this article until payment is collected.

3. If payment is by check, enter check number above.

4. Have customer sign Form 3849.

Follow proper scanning procedures for COD delivery and clearance.

20. Where would you indicate registered mail?
    (A) Box 1
    (B) Box 2
    (C) Box 3a
    (D) Box 3b

21. Where should the delivery date be entered?
    (A) Box 9
    (B) Box 10
    (C) Box 12
    (D) Box 13

22. What would be a correct entry for Box 5?
    (A) A checkmark
    (B) Henry Hines
    (C) August 1, 2008
    (D) Trenton, NJ 08618

23. According to the form, which of the following should be done?
    (A) The recipient should examine the contents before he or she pays the COD amount due.
    (B) The article can be delivered before payment is collected.
    (C) The customer should not sign Form 3849.
    (D) If the recipient pays by check, the check number should be entered on the form.

24. In which box should you check that the COD charges have been sent to the sender?
    (A) Box 3a
    (B) Box 3b
    (C) Box 4
    (D) Box 5

25. In which box should the money order number be entered?
    (A) Box 14
    (B) Box 11
    (C) Box 6
    (D) Box 2

Questions 26–30 are based on the following information.

REVERSE SIDE OF SORRY WE MISSED YOU	
We will redeliver OR you or your agent can pick up your mail at the post office. *(Bring this form and proper ID. If your agent will pick up, sign below in box 2, and enter agent's name here):*	
1. a. Check all that apply in box 3; b. Sign in box 2 below; c. Leave this notice where the carrier can see it.	**Delivery Section** **4.** Signature
2. Sign Here to Authorize Redelivery or to Authorize an Agent to Sign for You:	**5.** Printed Name
3a. ☐ Redeliver *(Enter day of week):* _____ (Allow at least two delivery days for redelivery, or call your post office to arrange delivery.) **3b.** ☐ Leave item at my address _____ (Specify where to leave. Example: "porch," "side door." This option is not available if box is checked on the front requiring your signature at time of delivery.) **3c.** ☐ Refused	**6.** Delivery Address

26. Where should the customer indicate that the customer wants someone to pick up the mail for him/her?
    (A) Box 1
    (B) Box 2
    (C) Box 4
    (D) Box 5

27. Which of these could be a correct entry for Box 3a?
    (A) Today
    (B) Wednesday
    (C) 10:00 A.M.
    (D) Next week

28. If Box 3b is checked, which of these is correct?
    (A) On the corner
    (B) In the kitchen
    (C) On the back porch
    (D) In the carrier's truck

29. Where should the customer leave the completed notice?
    (A) Where the carrier can see it
    (B) At the post office
    (C) On the customer's car windshield
    (D) In the mailbox on the corner

30. Where should the carrier indicate that the item is returned?
    (A) Box 3a
    (B) Box 3b
    (C) Box 3c
    (D) Box 6

PART C—CODING AND MEMORY

Section 1: Coding
6 Minutes
36 Questions

Directions: Assign a code to questions 1–36 based on the coding guide below.

CODING GUIDE	
Address Range	**Delivery Route**
801–1340 Fairleigh Rd. 1–149 Georgetown Ln.	A
3400–3699 Rowe Ave. 1341–1400 Fairleigh Rd. 150–299 Georgetown Ln.	B
12–92 Rock Run Dr. 2500–2700 Olympia Way 3700–4999 Rowe Ave.	C
All mail that doesn't fall in one of the address ranges listed above	D

	Address	Delivery Route			
1.	700 Fairleigh Rd.	A	B	C	D
2.	3607 Rowe Ave.	A	B	C	D
3.	34 Rock Run Dr.	A	B	C	D
4.	34 Georgetown Ln.	A	B	C	D
5.	1262 Olympia Way	A	B	C	D
6.	165 Georgetown Ln.	A	B	C	D
7.	4200 Rowe Ave.	A	B	C	D
8.	1500 Olympic Way	A	B	C	D

Address	Delivery Route			
9. 1401 Fairleigh Rd.	A	B	C	D
10. 132 Georgetown Ln.	A	B	C	D
11. 3400 Rowing Ave.	A	B	C	D
12. 1433 Fairleigh Rd.	A	B	C	D
13. 93 Rock Run Dr.	A	B	C	D
14. 149-C Georgetown Rd.	A	B	C	D
15. 1209 Fairleigh Rd.	A	B	C	D
16. 17 Rock Run Dr.	A	B	C	D
17. 5000 Rowe Ave.	A	B	C	D
18. 178 Georgetown Ln.	A	B	C	D
19. 2699 Olympia Way	A	B	C	D
20. 3456 Rowe Ave., Apt. 3C	A	B	C	D
21. 1400 Fairleigh Dickinson Rd.	A	B	C	D
22. 43 Rock Run Dr.	A	B	C	D
23. 989 Georgetown Ln.	A	B	C	D
24. 1365 Fairleigh Rd.	A	B	C	D
25. 3544 Rowe Ave.	A	B	C	D
26. 157-B Georgetown Ln.	A	B	C	D
27. 4533 Rowe Rd.	A	B	C	D
28. 800 Fairleigh Rd.	A	B	C	D
29. 3702 Rowe Ave.	A	B	C	D
30. 870 Georgetown Ln.	A	B	C	D
31. 43 Rock Run Dr.	A	B	C	D
32. 491 Georgetown Ln.	A	B	C	D
33. 1348 Fairleigh Rd.	A	B	C	D
34. 2576 Olympia Way	A	B	C	D
35. 159 Georgetown Rd.	A	B	C	D
36. 48 Rock Run Dr.	A	B	C	D

Section 2: Memory
7 Minutes
36 Questions

Directions: Take three minutes to memorize the coding guide below. Assign a code based on your memory of the coding guide. This coding guide is the same guide used in the previous coding section.

CODING GUIDE	
Address Range	**Delivery Route**
801–1340 Fairleigh Rd. 1–149 Georgetown Ln.	A
3400–3699 Rowe Ave. 1341–1400 Fairleigh Rd. 150–299 Georgetown Ln.	B
12–92 Rock Run Dr. 2500–2700 Olympia Way 3700–4999 Rowe Ave.	C
All mail that doesn't fall in one of the address ranges listed above	D

	Address	Delivery Route			
1.	43 Georgetown Ln.	A	B	C	D
2.	800 Fairleigh Rd.	A	B	C	D
3.	13 Rock Run Dr.	A	B	C	D
4.	2502 Olympia Way	A	B	C	D
5.	3700 Rowe Ave.	A	B	C	D
6.	154 Georgetown Ln.	A	B	C	D
7.	804 Fairleigh Rd.	A	B	C	D
8.	1544 Fairleigh Rd.	A	B	C	D

Address	Delivery Route			
9. 4300 Rowe Dr.	A	B	C	D
10. 152 Georgetown Ln.	A	B	C	D
11. 1433 Fairleigh Ave.	A	B	C	D
12. 43 Rock Run Dr.	A	B	C	D
13. 4333 Rowe Rd.	A	B	C	D
14. 156 Georgetown Ln.	A	B	C	D
15. 491 Georgetown Ln.	A	B	C	D
16. 3599 Rowe Ave.	A	B	C	D
17. 2677 Olympia Ave.	A	B	C	D
18. 3724 Rowe Ave.	A	B	C	D
19. 999 Fairleigh Rd.	A	B	C	D
20. 192 Rock Run Dr.	A	B	C	D
21. 132 Georgetown Ln.	A	B	C	D
22. 11 Rock Run Dr.	A	B	C	D
23. 4307 Rowe Dr.	A	B	C	D
24. 32 Georgetown Ln.	A	B	C	D
25. 2644 Olympia Way	A	B	C	D
26. 278 Georgetown Avenue	A	B	C	D
27. 1300 Fairleigh Rd.	A	B	C	D
28. 3999 Rowe Ave.	A	B	C	D
29. 210 Georgetown Ln.	A	B	C	D
30. 45 Rock Run Dr.	A	B	C	D
31. 3422 Olympic Way	A	B	C	D
32. 169 Georgetown Ln.	A	B	C	D
33. 76 Georgetown Ln.	A	B	C	D
34. 1347 Fairleigh Rd.	A	B	C	D
35. 4200 Rowe Ave.	A	B	C	D
36. 299 Georgetown Ln.	A	B	C	D

DIAGNOSTIC TEST ANSWER KEY

Part A—Address Checking

1.	D	21.	B	41.	A
2.	A	22.	B	42.	B
3.	B	23.	B	43.	B
4.	A	24.	B	44.	B
5.	B	25.	B	45.	B
6.	C A	26.	B	46.	A
7.	B	27.	A	47.	C
8.	A	28.	B	48.	A
9.	B	29.	B	49.	B
10.	D	30.	A	50.	B
11.	B	31.	A	51.	B
12.	B	32.	A	52.	A
13.	C	33.	A	53.	B
14.	A	34.	B	54.	A
15.	A	35.	B	55.	D
16.	B	36.	A	56.	B
17.	B	37.	A	57.	C
18.	D	38.	D	58.	A
19.	B	39.	B	59.	B
20.	A	40.	B	60.	B

Part B—Forms Completion

1.	C	7.	A	13.	C
2.	D	8.	B	14.	C
3.	A	9.	A	15.	D
4.	C	10.	C	16.	B
5.	B	11.	B	17.	A
6.	C	12.	D	18.	D

19.	A	23.	D	27.	B
20.	C	24.	D	28.	C
21.	B	25.	A	29.	A
22.	A	26.	B	30.	C

Part C—Coding and Memory

Section 1: Coding

1.	D	13.	D	25.	B
2.	B	14.	A	26.	B
3.	C	15.	A	27.	C
4.	A	16.	C	28.	D
5.	D	17.	D	29.	C
6.	B	18.	B	30.	D
7.	C	19.	A	31.	C
8.	D	20.	B	32.	D
9.	D	21.	D	33.	B
10.	A	22.	C	34.	C
11.	D	23.	D	35.	B
12.	D	24.	B	36.	C

Section 2: Memory

1.	A	13.	C	25.	C
2.	D	14.	B	26.	D
3.	C	15.	D	27.	A
4.	C	16.	B	28.	C
5.	C	17.	C	29.	B
6.	B	18.	B	30.	C
7.	A	19.	A	31.	D
8.	D	20.	D	32.	B
9.	C	21.	A	33.	A
10.	B	22.	D	34.	B
11.	D	23.	C	35.	C
12.	C	24.	A	36.	B

Strategies for Improving Your Address Checking

CHAPTER

3

STRATEGIES FOR IMPROVING YOUR ADDRESS CHECKING

3

Address Checking is the first part of Test 473. You do not really have to work faster than a speeding bullet, but you will have to work very fast, four seconds for each line. This chapter will help you build the skills needed to work at a quick yet accurate pace so you may score high on this portion of the exam. Take your time reviewing this chapter. The more time you devote to perfecting these techniques, the higher you can score on the exam.

GENERAL TEST STRATEGIES

As you learned in Chapter 1, address checking requires you to read and then compare two lines of addresses. Your best strategy for this part of the exam would be to *forget* most of the rules you have learned governing multiple-choice test taking.

Guessing

On this portion of the postal exam, you should *not* guess because the strategy for guessing will be different for the subsequent tests. Scoring procedures for this section take the number you have correct minus the number you have incorrect. The lines that you do not answer do not count in your score. Even though your odds for guessing the correct answer are pretty high, it is not beneficial to your score to guess. Stick with the answers you are fairly sure are correct; the odds are that you will have enough correct answers to get a good score. This is the only section in which it does not help to guess.

Address Checking is the only section in which it does not help to guess.

Reading

For this portion of the exam, it is a good idea to change your reading style. Many people have found the traditional way of reading—sounding out unknown words, possibly rereading misunderstood words, or reading at a rate good for comprehension—will not help them earn a high score. Instead of reading the addresses, master looking at them. You do not need to remember the address, so do not waste time trying to decipher strange street or city names. Look at their spelling and move on to the next. Precious time is wasted trying to sound out a name. It matters only if the street and city names are spelled similarly or differently.

For the Address Checking portion of the exam, it is a good idea to change your reading style.

Complete Accuracy

Your schoolteachers probably told you always to go for a perfect paper. A score of 100 was always the most desirable. Another strategy is to believe that getting every problem right is not always going to get you a higher score. Assume for a moment that you are in the middle of taking this exam. You work carefully on each line—so carefully that you get only three wrong. However, you finish only thirty problems. This gives you a score of 27 (number correct minus number incorrect). Your study partner works a bit faster, making six mistakes; however, he is able to complete forty problems. This means his score will be a 34, higher than yours, even though he got more incorrect answers. Slow and steady will not win this race. Expect to get a few wrong answers.

Attitude

A good attitude will supersede many shortcomings. If you review these strategies and techniques and believe that you can work fast and accurately, you probably will succeed. Imagine yourself sitting in the exam room, working quickly and accurately. On test day, as you are taking the exam, fit yourself into that picture.

TECHNIQUES FOR IMPROVING YOUR SKILLS

Setup

Every extra second counts, so follow these instructions carefully. Place your answer sheet at the edge of your test booklet so the pages line up perfectly. This will save time having to look across the desk to mark your answers. There will also be less time and distance to cause you to skip a line, whether on the test booklet or on your answer sheet. Working with the papers at a 90-degree angle in front of you may be uncomfortable at first. This is why you must practice this technique.

Hands

Your hands will keep you on track—as long as you do not let them wander. Hands naturally move slightly when a person moves his or her eyes or head to do another activity, say, marking an answer on an answer sheet. It is vital that you practice keeping your hands and head still, moving only your eyes.

Your hands should be relaxed and placed in front of you. Having your elbows at your sides with your wrists tense will not help. Place your left hand on the test booklet. The pinky finger should be on column A and the pointer finger should be on column D. As you move from line to line, simply slide your fingers down the page. Your arm never needs to move, only your fingers. By following this technique, you will save time having to look for your next line and avoid skipping over a line or looking at one twice. If, after practicing, you find this method too difficult, try using a

Exam Fact

It is vital that you practice keeping your hands and head still, moving only your eyes.

pencil as a straightedge. Rulers and other similar tools are not permitted in the exam room, but you are allowed to have an extra pencil. Why not use it to its greatest potential? Align the pencil under or over the line you are working on. Move the pencil down as you go. Again, this technique will save time because you will not have to check to see where your next line is. Practicing this technique will make it seem more natural come test day.

Do not forget the other hand. Your right hand should be placed lightly on the answer sheet. It should always be waiting at the number of the line you are comparing. By having your pencil marking the line, you will not have to waste valuable seconds looking for the line. There is also less chance of skipping a line or marking two answers on the same line. Remember to hold your pencil lightly and merely place it next to the number. This will keep your paper free of stray marks and your muscles more relaxed. This is no time for a cramp. Set your hands up while the examiner is going over the instructions.

To practice this technique before the day of the test, get two pieces of lined paper and a pencil. Make two columns on the one sheet to represent a test page. Place your fingers where they should go. Mark a column of numbers on the other page, representing answer lines. Practice moving your hands down a row as you pretend to look from paper to paper. When you feel comfortable holding your hands in these positions, try using the blank answer sheet provided instead of the lined paper. Remember to fill in the ovals with one quick swipe of the pencil. You are provided with answer rows running horizontally and vertically, so you may practice with both setups. As you progress, you should be able to fill in ninety-five ovals in approximately one minute's time.

Exam Fact

Remember to fill in the ovals with one quick swipe of the pencil.

A note to left-handers: There is a chance the answer sheet will be attached to the test booklet, making it necessary to fill in the answer with your right hand. Practice will help alleviate discomfort in using your right hand to fill in the ovals. When you drop off your admission form, ask about the setup your post office uses for materials.

Eyes

Eyes have a natural distance that they travel across a piece of written material. The eye looks at the written words in segments, with your muscles moving the eye from segment to segment. The length of each

Fast Fact

The eye looks at the written words in segments, with your muscles moving the eye from segment to segment.

segment is called eye span. You want to increase your eye span to the optimum length so you can see more in each segment that your eye moves. The more you see in each segment, the quicker you can compare each column. Here is an example of a short eye span. The lines separate the row to show each segment the eye sees.

/ 273 / Heathrow Dr. / Burdy, / IA /

To save time and energy, a better eye span would be as follows:

/ 273 Heathrow Dr. / Burdy, IA /

Once you have acquired an eye span of this length, try to see the whole line in just one sweep of the eye.

/ 273 Heathrow Dr. Burdy, IA /

Few people have an eye span this large, and acquiring one takes practice. There are some tricks and techniques to widen your eye span. Practice these slowly over time.

When you look at a group of words or letters, begin by looking toward the middle of the group. Let your peripheral vision see the beginning and ending letters. To practice catching more in one sweep, you will need index cards (or small strips of paper). In the middle of each card, place a black dot, large enough for your eye to catch it as you look at the card. Underneath each dot, write a line of words or numbers, being sure to center it under the black dot. Have a variety of line lengths—one-, two-, or three-word phrases—working your way to longer lines. Include many complete addresses like this: 489 Hobbey Way South. Choose four or five cards showing a line length with which you feel comfortable. Place them in a line or column in front of you. Practice reading the cards by focusing on the black dot and using your peripheral vision to take in the sides. A few examples have been modeled here for you.

Beginning
•
/ 489 /

Middle
•
/ 489 Hobbey /

Advanced

•

/ 489 Hobbey Way South /

This suggestion is *not* advice to look only at the middle numbers or words on the exam. Instead, these exercises are to widen your eye span. Working on peripheral vision is meant to increase your field of sight, which will help your speed on the exam. Later in this chapter, you will learn how to read all written work correctly.

Rhythm

Have you ever found yourself setting up a rhythm while you work? While painting a wall, you may dip the brush, wipe it off, stroke three times, dip the brush, wipe it off, stroke three times, and so on. Your movements become efficiently ingrained in your mind. A similar rhythm should be established while answering the address checking portion of the exam.

Exam Fact

If you want to earn a high score, you should compare two lines every four seconds.

If you want to earn a high score, you should compare two lines every four seconds. This is not a lot of time. To make sure that you truly are comparing two lines every four seconds, find a rhythm of moving to a new line every four seconds. With a watch, time the desired number of seconds you need to compare each line. At this point, you have a few options.

If you have been working on developing your eye span and feel comfortable sweeping the line in one movement, set your rhythm as follows. For each column, take one second to sweep, one second to look at your answer key, another second to mark your answer, and a fourth second to go back to the next line of comparisons. Count to yourself 1, 2, 3, 4 as you progress. Each step has a number. If you set up a rhythm, you can then work at fitting the act of comparing into the rhythm you have established. Remember, not everyone is expected to complete all of the comparisons, so if you need to take more time, do so. But be sure that you are completing enough comparisons correctly to give you a high score.

Exam Fact

Be sure that you are completing enough comparisons correctly to give you a high score.

Correct Looking

In the previous section, it was suggested that you simply look at the addresses rather than read them. To be sure you are not wasting time trying to sound out funny words or make sense of strange abbreviations, read the words or numbers exactly as they are printed. Here are some examples:

104	One oh four
Dr.	Dee Ahr
NJ	En Jay

This will save you from overlooking a simple change. The brain functions by automatically filling in missing parts. If you did not make yourself conscious of a letter change in a state abbreviation, your brain will probably overlook it and fill in what it feels is correct.

Sound out each syllable when you look at street addresses. This will make you conscious of smaller chunks, and it will make it easier to pick out a wrong letter in the middle of a word. For instance, "Cornwall" would be seen as "Corn-wall." Practice saying these addresses as suggested.

9024, 384, 1002, 3920, 5578, 29, 1582
St., Ct., Ave., Pl., S., W., N., E., Terr.
IA, CA, NY, AL, WY, WA

Common Changes

Studies have shown the following are common changes in addresses. Be aware of these changes so you can expect them. Your eyes may make changes for you, even if they are not on paper.

Letter reversals: b/d, a/o, a/e, m/w, n/m, p/e, q/d, u/n, u/v
Parts of names: Walker, Walk, Waller, Walken, Wilken
Number reversals: 478, 487, 748, 847, 784, 874

To practice recognizing these changes, prepare index cards with a number, name, or letter on one side and, on the other side, either the same figure or a slight variation. Quickly turn the card over, not looking at it for more than a second or two. State whether it is the same or different. If you want to brush up on your stroking technique, use a blank answer sheet to fill in A or D.

Here are two drills to help you differentiate between number and name reversals. Mark the number space in which you saw the word. If you did not see the exact word repeated, mark a zero. You may want to repeat this exercise periodically to keep the technique fresh in your mind.

	1	2	3	4	5	
1. Boyton	Boyon	Boyton	Boytun	Boyten	Bayton	_____
2. Leary	Learry	Laary	Leavy	Leary	Lerry	_____
3. Sporten	Spoten	Sportan	Sgorten	Sporten	Sgortan	_____
4. Kline	Klinn	Klime	Klina	Klima	Kliwe	_____
5. Gelinas	Galinas	Gellnas	Gelinas	Gelinns	Gilenas	_____
6. Griego	Qriego	Griego	Griago	Griega	Qrigo	_____
7. Avacedo	Avacebo	Awacedo	Avacado	Avaceda	Avacedo	_____
8. Kessler	Kezzler	Kessler	Kassler	Kesslr	Kesselr	_____
9. Lipton	Lidton	Libton	Lijton	Lipten	Lipton	_____
10. Dobde	Dodbe	Dobda	Dobdo	Dodbo	Dobde	_____

	Answer Grid				
1.	①	●	③	④	⑤
2.	①	②	③	●	⑤
3.	①	②	③	●	⑤
4.	①	②	③	④	⑤
5.	①	②	●	④	⑤
6.	①	●	③	④	⑤
7.	①	②	③	④	●
8	①	●	③	④	⑤
9.	①	②	③	④	●
10.	①	②	③	④	●

		1	2	3	4	5	
1.	489	849	489	494	498	499	_____
2	2904	2900	2940	2904	2094	2099	_____
3.	5918	5918	5198	5988	5919	5198	_____
4.	6643	6443	6634	6644	6646	6643	_____
5.	1001	1000	1010	1100	1001	1011	_____
6.	2189	2891	2981	2189	2991	2198	_____
7.	7791	7991	7191	7197	7719	7791	_____
8.	3357	3557	3551	3531	3775	3357	_____
9.	11010	10110	01101	11010	00110	10101	_____
10.	696	969	696	669	969	996	_____

	Answer Grid				
1.	①	●	③	④	⑤
2.	①	②	●	④	⑤
3.	●	②	③	④	⑤
4.	①	②	③	④	●
5.	①	②	③	●	⑤
6.	①	②	●	④	⑤
7.	①	②	③	④	●
8	①	②	③	④	●
9.	①	②	●	④	⑤
10.	①	●	③	④	⑤

Looking Back

Do not fall into the trap of looking back to check your work. Many people feel the urgent need to look over the addresses one last time. If you had all day, this would be fine, but remember you have only a few seconds for each one. Once you have made your initial sweeps, move on. For those who like to be meticulous, this may be difficult. Here are two exercises to break you of the habit of looking back.

Exam Fact

Do not fall into the trap of looking back to check your work.

Take a piece of paper folded lengthwise to form a rectangle. Use this to cover the written text above the line you are working on. Use your left hand to move the paper down as you go. Obviously, this won't work if you are correctly marking your lines with your fingers. Until you no longer feel the need to look back, forsake holding your spot with your fingers. Let the paper mark your spot. As you become more comfortable sticking with your original answer, you can wean yourself away from using the paper cover.

If you tend to look back only at column A when you should be looking at column B, use an index card to cover the column. An index card can be moved easily to allow you to scan the next line when you need to, but it can cover the column once you have scanned the appropriate information.

Three practice exercises follow. Each exercise gets a bit harder. Ninety-five comparisons have been given so you can become familiar with the length of the exam section. Review the techniques described in these pages. Continue to work on and use these techniques as you complete these exercises. Practice will make them seem like second nature.

Continue with three practice exercises, each with ninety-five comparisons. The first should be only numbers, the second numbers and streets, and the third a combination of the first two and state abbreviations and ZIP codes.

DRILL: ADDRESS CHECKING WITH NUMBERS ONLY

			SAME	DIFFERENT
1.	3215	3125	A	D
2.	4001	4001	A	D
3.	5931	5931	A	D
4.	32187	32178	A	D
5.	08842	08842	A	D
6.	74123	74123	A	D
7.	67	67	A	D
8.	2331	2332	A	D
9.	07512	07512	A	D
10.	110	1100	A	D
11.	51620	51620	A	D

			SAME	DIFFERENT
12.	43102	43101	A	D
13.	98714	97814	A	D
14.	4233	4322	A	D
15.	37430	37431	A	D
16.	10112	11012	A	D
17.	40213	40213	A	D
18.	9893	9893	A	D
19.	31021	31021	A	D
20.	59710	57910	A	D
21.	7529	7259	A	D
22.	2941	294	A	D
23.	00145	00143	A	D
24.	3102	3120	A	D
25.	157	167	A	D
26.	20014	20015	A	D
27.	23419	23459	A	D
28.	485	486	A	D
29.	10529	10929	A	D
30.	14209	14209	A	D
31.	3391	3191	A	D
32.	52018	52018	A	D
33.	36210	36210	A	D
34.	98213	98213	A	D
35.	42189	42189	A	D
36.	0227	02272	A	D
37.	6003	6008	A	D
38.	973	373	A	D
39.	12203	12203	A	D
40.	49513	49518	A	D
41.	42038	42038	A	D
42.	78421	78421	A	D
43.	57892	57392	A	D
44.	32095	32005	A	D
45.	43215	42315	A	D
46.	90542	90452	A	D
47.	86832	86632	A	D
48.	95031	95031	A	D
49.	13922	13222	A	D

			SAME	DIFFERENT
50.	208	208	A	D
51.	4096	4069	A	D
52.	4409-2348	4409-2348	A	D
53.	4864	4854	A	D
54.	37034	37035	A	D
55.	376	374	A	D
56.	84563	84566	A	D
57.	4862	4862	A	D
58.	694	694	A	D
59.	64920	64820	A	D
60.	482	482	A	D
61.	49135	49135	A	D
62.	79013	97013	A	D
63.	9465	9465	A	D
64.	48210	48210	A	D
65.	2384	2334	A	D
66.	593	593	A	D
67.	872	872	A	D
68.	76	76	A	D
69.	3947-6492	3947-6942	A	D
70.	5934	5934	A	D
71.	49892	49892	A	D
72.	4823	4328	A	D
73.	38107	38107	A	D
74.	53267	53267	A	D
75.	28103	24103	A	D
76.	794	794	A	D
77.	8524	8224	A	D
78.	46954	6950	A	D
79.	05681	05681	A	D
80.	582	582	A	D
81.	493	493	A	D
82.	71905	7190	A	D
83.	46824	46824	A	D
84.	31824	31824	A	D
85.	39640	3964	A	D
86.	9462	94621	A	D

		SAME	DIFFERENT
87. 38	381	A	D
88. 46722	46742	A	D
89. 3664	3646	A	D
90. 548770	584770	A	D
91. 463	4631	A	D
92. 4568	4568	A	D
93. 734	0734	A	D
94. 46823	46823	A	D
95. 95237	95237	A	D

ANSWERS TO DRILL:
ADDRESS CHECKING WITH NUMBERS ONLY

1. D	20. D	39. A	58. A	77. D
2. A	21. D	40. D	59. D	78. D
3. A	22. D	41. A	60. A	79. A
4. D	23. D	42. A	61. A	80. A
5. A	24. D	43. D	62. D	81. A
6. A	25. D	44. D	63. A	82. D
7. A	26. D	45. D	64. A	83. A
8. D	27. D	46. D	65. D	84. A
9. A	28. D	47. D	66. A	85. D
10. D	29. D	48. A	67. A	86. D
11. A	30. A	49. D	68. A	87. D
12. D	31. D	50. A	69. D	88. D
13. D	32. A	51. D	70. A	89. D
14. D	33. A	52. A	71. A	90. D
15. D	34. A	53. D	72. D	91. D
16. D	35. A	54. D	73. A	92. A
17. A	36. D	55. D	74. A	93. D
18. A	37. D	56. D	75. D	94. A
19. A	38. D	57. A	76. A	95. A

DRILL: ADDRESS CHECKING WITH NUMBERS AND STREET NAMES

			SAME	DIFFERENT
1.	2112 Hilltop Road	1221 Hilltop Road	A	D
2.	34 Blossom Trail Road	34 Blossom Trail Avenue	A	D
3.	450 Chester Ct.	45 Chester Ct.	A	D
4.	30 Saddle River Dr.	30 Saddle River Dr.	A	D
5.	89 W. Fifteenth Ave. E	89 W. Fiftieth Ave. E	A	D
6.	First & Main	First & Main	A	D
7.	234 Thousand Oaks	234 Thousand Oaks	A	D
8.	26 Apt. 5I Tenth Ave.	26 Apt. 5K Tenth Ave.	A	D
9.	10012 Square Mill Run	10012 Square Mill Run	A	D
10.	450 Hudson Apt. 52	450 Hudson Apt. S2	A	D
11.	49 JFK Blvd.	49 JFK Blvd.	A	D
12.	764 Shadowbrook	764 Shadowbrook	A	D
13.	420 Lafayette	420 Lafayette	A	D
14.	99 Harvard Street Apt. 3	99 Harvard Street Apt. 3	A	D
15.	8200 Tulane Street	820 Tulane Street	A	D
16.	2193 Georges Avenue	2193 George Avenue	A	D
17.	83 Washington Blvd.	83 Washington St.	A	D
18.	732 Hunter's Mill	732 Hunter's Mill Run	A	D
19.	84 Freeman Street	841 Freeman Street	A	D
20.	30 Langford Drive	30 Lanford Drive	A	D
21.	586 Broadway	586 W. Broadway	A	D
22.	42 Green Street	42 Greene Street	A	D
23.	71 Prince Avenue	71 Prince Avenue	A	D
24.	485 Mark Drive	485 Mark Drive	A	D
25.	55 Ludlow Street Apt. 3D	55 Ludlow Street Apt. 3D	A	D
26.	91 Sonoma Place	91 Somona Place	A	D
27.	66 Freeland Ave.	66 Frieland Ave.	A	D
28.	18 Lori Drive	18 Lorry Drive	A	D
29.	72 Beaumont Place	72 Beaumonte Place	A	D
30.	35 Plainsville Road	35 Plainsview Road	A	D
31.	27 Mountainview Drive	27 Mountainside Drive	A	D
32.	87 Longley Terr.	87 Longley Terr.	A	D
33.	49 Martin Blvd.	49 Martin Blvd.	A	D
34.	62 Demot Lane	62 Demott Lane	A	D

			SAME	DIFFERENT
35.	23 Amwell Drive East	23 Amwell Drive East	A	D
36.	75 E. Broad Street	75 W. Broad Street	A	D
37.	9067 Lyde Avenue	9076 Lyde Avenue	A	D
38.	8213 Vert Road	8213 Vert Road	A	D
39.	78 Franklin Blvd.	78 Franklin Blvd.	A	D
40.	63 Rock Lake Circle	63 Rock Lake Circle	A	D
41.	42 Fort Wayne Drive	42 Fort Wayne Drive	A	D
42.	PO Box 4063	PO Box 4063	A	D
43.	76 Longfellow Drive	76 Longefellow Drive	A	D
44.	928 Beford Street	928 Medford Street	A	D
45.	729 Deal Place	729 Deal Place	A	D
46.	937 Black Terr.	937 Black Terr.	A	D
47.	7650 Deland St.	7650 Dealand St.	A	D
48.	8420 Seventh Ave.	8420 Seventh St.	A	D
49.	8983 MacGregor Pl.	8983 McGregor Pl.	A	D
50.	451 Highland Dr.	451 Highland Dr.	A	D
51.	6243 US Hwy. No.1	6243 US Hwy. No.1	A	D
52.	7459 Durham Avenue	745 Durham Avenue	A	D
53.	834 Edwards Blvd.	834 Edward Blvd.	A	D
54.	7840 King Pl.	7840 King Pl.	A	D
55.	67 Prospect Ave. Apt. 3	67 Prospect Ave. Apt. 3F	A	D
56.	985 Foxwood Road	885 Foxwood Road	A	D
57.	33 Causeway	333 Causeway	A	D
58.	401 N. Main St. Apt. 5H	401 S. Main St. Apt. 5H	A	D
59.	S Park & Adams	S Park & Adam	A	D
60.	7789 Morris Ave.	7789 Morris Ave.	A	D
61.	889 Handy St.	8889 Handy St.	A	D
62.	789 Parsonage Rd.	789 Parsonage Rd.	A	D
63.	76 Redmond St.	76 Readmond St.	A	D
64.	74921 Amboy Blvd.	74921 Amboy Blvd.	A	D
65.	797 Hamliton Drive	797 Hamilton Drive	A	D
66.	US Hwy. No. 18	US Hwy. No. 18	A	D
67.	831 Morgan Rd.	831 Morgan Rd.	A	D
68.	4447 Dayton Drive	4477 Dayton Drive	A	D
69.	9421 Ryan Road Apt. 2	9412 Ryan Road Apt. 2	A	D
70.	49 Mill Run Road	493 Mill Run Road	A	D
71.	1510 Stelton Street	1015 Stelton Street	A	D
72.	225 Madison Ave.	225 Madison Ave.	A	D

			SAME	DIFFERENT
73.	11 Alvin Court	11 Alvin Court	A	D
74.	888 Railroad Drive	88 Railroad Drive	A	D
75.	667 French Street	667 French Street	A	D
76.	6775 Woodside Rd.	6775 Woodside Rd.	A	D
77.	597 Nassau St.	597 Nassau St.	A	D
78.	7546 Route 518	7456 Route 518	A	D
79.	56 Myrtle Drive	56 Myrtle Drive	A	D
80.	662 Ford Ave.	662 Fords Ave.	A	D
81.	2263 Baldwin Drive	226S Baldwin Drive	A	D
82.	20 Rose St.	20 Rose St.	A	D
83.	6646 Ray St.	6664 Ray St.	A	D
84.	8872 Duchamp Drive	8872 Duchamp Drive	A	D
85.	2135 Route 1	2135 Route 1	A	D
86.	84 North Avenue	845 North Avenue	A	D
87.	Main & Water	Main & Water	A	D
88.	775 Pfieffer Blvd.	771 Pfieffer Blvd.	A	D
89.	6732 Lawrence St.	6732 Lawrence St.	A	D
90.	34 White Oak Lane	34 White Oak Lane	A	D
91.	6 Patrick Blvd.	6 Patrick Blvd.	A	D
92.	US Hwy. No. 13 S.	US Hwy. No. 130	A	D
93.	84 Cotter Drive	48 Cotter Drive	A	D
94.	370 Ridge Road	307 Ridge Road	A	D
95.	541 E. Hazlewood Dr.	541 W. Hazlewood Dr.	A	D

ANSWERS TO DRILL: ADDRESS CHECKING WITH NUMBERS AND STREET NAMES

1.	D	10.	D	19.	D	28.	D	37.	D
2.	D	11.	A	20.	D	29.	D	38.	A
3.	D	12.	A	21.	D	30.	D	39.	A
4.	A	13.	A	22.	D	31.	D	40.	A
5.	D	14.	A	23.	A	32.	A	41.	A
6.	A	15.	D	24.	A	33.	A	42.	A
7.	A	16.	D	25.	A	34.	D	43.	D
8.	D	17.	D	26.	D	35.	A	44.	D
9.	A	18.	D	27.	D	36.	D	45.	A

46.	A	56.	D	66.	A	76.	A	86.	D
47.	D	57.	D	67.	A	77.	A	87.	A
48.	D	58.	D	68.	D	78.	D	88.	D
49.	A	59.	D	69.	D	79.	A	89.	A
50.	A	60.	A	70.	D	80.	D	90.	A
51.	A	61.	D	71.	D	81.	D	91.	A
52.	D	62.	A	72.	A	82.	A	92.	D
53.	D	63.	D	73.	A	83.	D	93.	D
54.	A	64.	A	74.	D	84.	A	94.	D
55.	D	65.	D	75.	A	85.	A	95.	D

DRILL: FULL ADDRESS CHECKING

			SAME	DIFFERENT
1.	776 Circle Ave.	776 Circle Ave.	A	D
2.	111 Paulison Road	1111 Paulison Road	A	D
3.	80 Mattison Ave.	80 Mattison Ave.	A	D
4.	37 Minnisink Drive	37 Minnisink Drive	A	D
5.	New York, NY	New York, NJ	A	D
6.	1020 Circe Ave.	1020 Circle Ave.	A	D
7.	349 Pier Lane Apt. 34	3490 Pier Lane Apt. 34	A	D
8.	27 Ellison Drive	27 Ellison Drive	A	D
9.	55 Fairview Drive	55 Fairlawn Drive	A	D
10.	114 Beach Parkway	114 Beach Parkway	A	D
11.	426 Fern Terr.	426 Fern Drive	A	D
12.	1001 Bethl Road W.	101 Bethl Road W.	A	D
13.	Mtn. View, CA 94040	Mtn. View, CA 95040	A	D
14.	26 Lackawanna Ave.	26 Lackawanna Ave.	A	D
15.	251 Belmont	251 Belmont Apt. 1	A	D
16.	38 Sunset Drive	38 Sunset Drive	A	D
17.	4428 Manchester Road	4248 Manchester Road	A	D
18.	748 Barclay Court	748 Barclay Court	A	D
19.	134 Hamburg Drive	134 Hapsburg Drive	A	D
20.	71 Wooley Ave.	71 Woodley Ave.	A	D
21.	8 Burlington Drive	8 Burlington Drive	A	D

			SAME	DIFFERENT
22.	34 Grand St.	34 Grand St.	A	D
23.	4226 Brookside Dr.	426 Brookside Dr.	A	D
24.	1030 Doremus La.	1030 Dormus Lane	A	D
25.	33 E. Second St.	33 W. Second St.	A	D
26.	Clifton, NJ 07012	Clifton, NJ 07012	A	D
27.	17 Pequannock Dr.	17 Pequannock Dr.	A	D
28.	896 Lee Avenue	896 Leigh Avenue	A	D
29.	34 Robertson Drive	34 Robertsen Drive	A	D
30.	79 Elizabeth Pl.	79 Elizabeth Pl	A	D
31.	22 Little Falls Rd.	22 Little Falls Rd.	A	D
32.	36 Berry Drive	46 Berry Drive	A	D
33.	1173 Goffle St.	11173 Goffle St. W.	A	D
34.	3050 State Hwy. No. 280	3050 State Hwy. No. 280	A	D
35.	117 Westervelt Ave.	117 Westerbelt Ave	A	D
36.	Chelsea, MA 02150	Chelsea, MD 02550	A	D
37.	59 Elmwood Park Apt. 2	59 Elmwood Park Apt. 2	A	D
38.	7801 Burlington Drive	7801 Burlington Drive	A	D
39.	4021 N Haledon St.	4021 S Haldeon St.	A	D
40.	44501 Union Ave.	44501 Union Ave.	A	D
41.	159 Paterson Ave.	195 Paterson Ave.	A	D
42.	5 Lorelei Drive Apt. 55	5 Lorelei Drive Apt 5S	A	D
43.	77 E. Garden Pl.	77 W. Garden Pl.	A	D
44.	Glendale, AZ 85306	Glendale, AZ 85306	A	D
45.	100 Busse Ln.	100 Bussel Ln.	A	D
46.	17 Iowa Avenue	170 Iowa Avenue	A	D
47.	65 S Kinellon Ave.	65 S Kinelon Ave.	A	D
48.	157 Valley Road	167 Valley Road	A	D
49.	7901 Ackerman Ct.	7901 Ackerman Ct.	A	D
50.	264 US Hwy. No. 46	2644 US Hwy. No. 46	A	D
51.	88 Forest Road S.	888 Forest Road S.	A	D
52.	Brooklyn, NY 11211	Brooklyn, NY 11231	A	D
53.	831 Kajiawara Drive	831 Kajiawara Drive	A	D
54.	505 Court St.	5005 Court St.	A	D
55.	63 H Street Apt. 4A	631 H Street Apt. 4A	A	D
56.	151 Bergenline Ave.	15 Bergenline Ave.	A	D
57.	47 McBride Drive	47 McBride Drive	A	D
58.	110 Kipp Avenue	1110 Kipp Avenue	A	D
59.	77-1 Alabama Drive	77-1 Alabama Drive	A	D

			SAME	DIFFERENT
60.	274 Haledon Avenue	274 Haldon Avenue	A	D
61.	1240 Tonnelle Avenue S	1240 Tonnelle Avenue S	A	D
62.	Houston, TX 77019	Houston, TX 77019	A	D
63.	669 Park Slope Blvd.	699 Park Slope Blvd.	A	D
64.	475 Crooks Ave.	475 Cook Ave.	A	D
65.	250 Berdan Ave. Apt. 55	250 Berdan Ave. Apt. 5D	A	D
66.	14-33 Plaza Blvd.	14-33 Plaza Blvd.	A	D
67.	216 Ellis Blvd.	216 Eli Blvd.	A	D
68.	E-2110 State Hwy. No. 6	W-2210 State Hwy. No 6	A	D
69.	400 Bushes Lane	4000 Bushes Lane	A	D
70.	410 Fifth Ave. Apt. 22	410 Fifth Ave. Apt. 22	A	D
71.	155 Willowbrook Terr.	155 Willowbrook Terr.	A	D
72.	55 Colfax Drive	55 Colfax Drive	A	D
73.	932 Piaget Ave.	932 Piage Ave.	A	D
74.	1112 Peakness Avenue	112 Peakness Avenue	A	D
75.	8 Doig Rd.	8 Dog Rd.	A	D
76.	Bowling Green, OH 43402	Bowling Green, OK 43402	A	D
77.	22 Sandcastle Drive	223 Sandcastle Drive	A	D
78.	1121 Key Street	1121 Key Street	A	D
79.	8833 Church Street	8833 Church Street	A	D
80.	15 Summit Ave.	15 Summit Ave.	A	D
81.	77 Essex Road	770 Essex Road	A	D
82.	4 Bramar Drive	4 Braemar Drive	A	D
83.	Elkridge, MD 21227	Elkridge, MD 21227	A	D
84.	122 Parish Drive Apt. 44	122 Parish Drive Apt. 12	A	D
85.	US Hwy. No. 16 & US Hwy. No. 34	US Hwy. No. 16 & US. Hwy. No. 33	A	D
86.	88 Broad Avenue	88 Broadview	A	D
87.	San Francisco, CA 94110	San Francisco, CA 94111	A	D
88.	1 Station Road	11 Station Road	A	D
89.	Boulder, CO 80306	Boulder, CO 80306	A	D
90.	6643 Notch Ct.	7743 Notch Ct.	A	D
91.	Carboro, NC 27510	Carrboro, NC 27510	A	D
92.	221 Emery Dr.	221 Emery Ave.	A	D
93.	5458 Alps Drive	5485 Alps Drive	A	D
94.	20 Onyx Terr.	20 Onyx Terr.	A	D
95.	Orlando, FL 32801	Orlando, FL 32802	A	D

ANSWERS TO DRILL: FULL ADDRESS CHECKING

1. A	20. D	39. D	58. D	77. D
2. D	21. A	40. A	59. A	78. A
3. A	22. A	41. D	60. D	79. A
4. A	23. D	42. D	61. A	80. A
5. D	24. D	43. D	62. A	81. D
6. D	25. D	44. A	63. D	82. D
7. D	26. A	45. D	64. D	83. A
8. A	27. A	46. D	65. D	84. D
9. D	28. D	47. D	66. A	85. D
10. A	29. D	48. D	67. D	86. D
11. D	30. A	49. A	68. D	87. D
12. D	31. A	50. D	69. D	88. D
13. D	32. D	51. D	70. A	89. A
14. A	33. D	52. D	71. A	90. D
15. D	34. A	53. A	72. A	91. D
16. A	35. D	54. D	73. D	92. D
17. D	36. D	55. D	74. D	93. D
18. A	37. A	56. D	75. D	94. A
19. D	38. A	57. A	76. D	95. D

Strategies for Improving Your Forms Completion Skills

STRATEGIES FOR IMPROVING YOUR FORMS COMPLETION SKILLS

4

Part B, "Forms Completion," contains thirty questions in which you are tested on your ability to identify the information you need to complete the forms that are similar to those used by the Postal Service. Because this section requires some thought, you are given fifteen minutes to finish, which is a bit more time than that allotted for the other sections. You will be given several forms with questions about what information you need to complete each of the forms. The forms are labeled as boxes, for example, Box 1, Box 1a, Box 3b, and the like. Because you are given approximately thirty seconds to answer each question, you must work quickly and accurately. If you do not know an answer, make an educated guess because no points are deducted for wrong answers on this part of the test. You should try not to skip a question without making a guess. On the other hand, you should not spend too much time on a question for which the answer is not readily apparent to you. If you do skip a few questions and find you have some extra time before the time for the test is up, go back and fill in any guesses in order to finish the section.

Exam Fact

You should try not to skip a question without making a guess.

GENERAL TEST STRATEGIES

Guessing

In this section, guessing will not penalize you the way it would in the Address Checking section. However, if you practice the techniques in this chapter and develop a rhythm, you should not have to guess very often. You should have time to go back to any problems you may have skipped.

Filling in Answers

You can use the fact that you have time to scrutinize the answers to your advantage. If you become stuck on a question and have time remaining, start filling in the answer choices.

Keep with Your Rhythm

By now, you should be aware of the advantage of developing a rhythm on timed tests; it will be important for determining the amount of time you can allot to each question. If you find yourself out of the rhythm during the exam, you may be spending too much time on difficult questions.

TECHNIQUES FOR IMPROVING YOUR SKILLS

Carefully Study Each Form

Exam Fact

You will find that each of the Postal Service forms is different.

You will find that each of the Postal Service forms is different. Make sure you read the forms before you start to answer the questions so you know what information is expected. First, skim the entire form. Usually, it's not that long. Skimming will give you a general idea of the contents. Then carefully read the entire form until you are certain that you understand the details.

Answer the Questions You Know First

If you have to return to a question, make sure you are careful in marking the correct answer on your answer sheet. When you skip questions, it is very easy to find yourself in the wrong place on the answer sheet and fill in the wrong oval.

Remember, if you have enough time, make sure you go back and attempt the difficult items and make an educated guess.

 DRILL: FORMS COMPLETION PRACTICE

Directions: Read each form and answer the questions based on the information provided.

Questions 1–5 are based on the following information.

SIGNATURE CONFIRMATION RECEIPT	
Postage and Signature Confirmation fees must be paid before mailing.	
1. Name	**2.** Street Address
3. City and State	**4.** Waiver of Signature ☐ YES ☐ NO
5. Postmark Here	**6a.** ☐ Priority Mail™ Service **6b.** ☐ First-Class Mail® parcel **6c.** ☐ Package Services parcel

7a. ☐ WAIVER OF SIGNATURE
   If addressee or addressee's agent is not available to sign for delivery, I authorize that the delivery employee's signature constitutes valid proof of delivery if the item can be left in a secure location.

7b. CUSTOMER SIGNATURE _____

1. Where should a name be entered on this form?

    (A) Box 1

    (B) Box 2

    (C) Box 3

    (D) Box 4

2. Which of these is a correct entry for Box 4?

    (A) $3.98

    (B) 2008

    (C) A postmark

    (D) A check mark

3. Where would you enter the sender's street address?

    (A) Box 2

    (B) Box 5

    (C) Box 4

    (D) Box 7b

4. You could enter a checkmark in each of the following boxes EXCEPT

    (A) 6a.

    (B) 6b.

    (C) 6c.

    (D) 7b.

5. Where would you indicate that the signature will be waived?

    (A) Boxes 1 and 2

    (B) Boxes 4 and 7

    (C) Boxes 5 and 6a

    (D) Boxes 6b and 7b

Questions 6–11 are based on the following information.

ATTEMPTED DELIVERY NOTICE	
SENDER: *COMPLETE THIS SECTION*	*COMPLETE THIS SECTION ON DELIVERY*
■ Complete boxes 1, 2, and 3. Also complete box 4 if Restricted Delivery is desired. ■ Print your name and address on the reverse so that we can return the card to you. ■ Attach this card to the back of the mailpiece, or on the front if space permits. **1.** Article Addressed to:	**A.** Signature **X** □ Agent □ Addressee
	B. Received by *(Printed Name)* **C.** Date of Delivery
	D. Is delivery address different from item 1? If YES, enter delivery address below: □ Yes □ No
	3. Service Type 3a. □ Certified Mail 3d. □ Express Mail 3b. □ Registered 3e. □ Return Receipt for Merchandise 3c. □ Insured Mail 3f. □ C.O.D.
2. Article Number *(Transfer from service label)*	**4.** Restricted Delivery? *(Extra Fee)* □ Yes

6. Which of these would be a correct entry for Box C?

   (A) $3.98

   (B) 11/23/08

   (C) 502 Main St.

   (D) Chicago, IL 60612

7. Where would you enter the article number?

   (A) Box 1

   (B) Box 2

   (C) Box 3

   (D) Box 4

8. Where would you indicate that the customer wants to send this article by Express Mail?

   (A) Box D

   (B) Box 3b

   (C) Box 3d

   (D) Box 4

9. Which of these would be a correct entry for Box 4?

   (A) The customer's signature

   (B) Jeanne Warrick

   (C) 45678

   (D) A checkmark

10. Where would you enter the address if the delivery address is different from item 1?

    (A) Box D

    (B) Box 1

    (C) Box 2

    (D) Box 4

11. In which box would you indicate that the article was received?

    (A) Box 2

    (B) Box A

    (C) Box B

    (D) Box D

Questions 12–16 are based on the following information.

RETURN RECEIPT FOR MERCHANDISE

(Domestic Mail Only; No Insurance Coverage Provided)

OFFICIAL USE

1. Postage $	**6.** Postmark Here
2. Return Receipt for Merchandise Fee (Endorsement Required)	
3. Special Handling Fee	
4. Total Postage & Fees $	
5. Waiver Signature ☐ YES ☐ NO	

7. *Sent To*

8. *Street, Apt. No.*
or PO Box No.

9. *City, State, ZIP+4*

10. ☐ WAIVER OF SIGNATURE
I wish delivery to be made without obtaining signature of the addressee or the addressee's agent. I authorize the delivery employee to sign that the shipment was delivered and understand that the signature of the delivery employee will constitute valid proof of delivery.

_____

CUSTOMER SIGNATURE

12. Where would you indicate the return receipt fee?

    (A) Box 1

    (B) Box 2

    (C) Box 3

    (D) Box 4

13. Which of these would be a correct entry for Box 9?

    (A) 72 Parkside Ave.

    (B) Philadelphia

    (C) Pennsylvania

    (D) Philadelphia, PA 12315-7272

14. You could enter a dollar amount in each of the following boxes EXCEPT

    (A) Box 1.

    (B) Box 3.

    (C) Box 4.

    (D) Box 6.

15. In which of the following boxes would a checkmark and a signature be correct entries?

    (A) Box 10

    (B) Box 5

    (C) Box 3

    (D) Box 1

16. In which box would you indicate the post office postmark?

    (A) Box 5

    (B) Box 6

    (C) Box 7

    (D) Box 10

Questions 17–21 are based on the following information.

RECEIPT FOR REGISTERED MAIL	
To Be Completed By Post Office	
1. Reg. Fee	
2. Handling Charge	**4.** Return Receipt
3. Postage	**5.** Restricted Delivery
6. Received by	
7. Customer Must Declare Full Value $ Domestic Insurance up to $25,000 is included based upon the declared value. International Indemnity is limited. *(See Reverse).*	**8.** Date Stamp
OFFICIAL USE	
To Be Completed By Customer (Please Print) **All Entries Must Be In Ballpoint Pen or Typed**	
9. FROM	
10. TO	

17. If the full value of the package is $310, where would you indicate this?
    (A) Box 1
    (B) Box 3
    (C) Box 6
    (D) Box 7

18. Carol Slaughter is sending the package to 1234 Toad Lane. Where would you enter the street address?
    (A) Box 10
    (B) Box 9
    (C) Box 8
    (D) Box 7

19. Where would you indicate that you have received the package for delivery?
    (A) Box 6
    (B) Box 7
    (C) Box 9
    (D) Box 10

20. Which of these would be a correct entry for Box 7?
    (A) A checkmark
    (B) The postmark
    (C) A signature
    (D) A dollar amount

21. The postal clerk completes all of the following boxes EXCEPT
    (A) Box 2.
    (B) Box 6.
    (C) Box 8.
    (D) Box 9.

Questions 22–30 are based on the following information.

COD		
Collect the amount shown below, if customer pays by CHECK made payable to the mailer.	**Collect the amount shown below if customer pays in CASH** *(Includes MO fee or fees).*	
1. Check Amount $	**2.** Cash Amount $	
3. ☐ Registered Mail ☐ Express Mail® Service ☐ Form 3849-D Requested		
4. Date of Mailing	**5.** ☐ Remit COD Charges to Sender via Express Mail	**6.** EMCA No.
7. From:	**8.** To:	
9. Delivered By	**10.** Date Delivered	**11.** Check Number
12. Date Payment Sent to Mailer	**13.** Date Form 3849-D Sent	**14.** MO Number(s)

1. DO NOT allow the recipient *(addressee or agent)* to examine the contents before payment.

2. DO NOT deliver this article until payment is collected.

3. If payment is by check, enter check number above.

4. Have customer sign Form 3849.

   Follow proper scanning procedures for COD delivery and clearance.

22. Which of these would be a correct entry for Box 11?

    (A) $67.98

    (B) 08540

    (C) #101

    (D) 12/25/08

23. Where would you indicate that the COD amount was paid in cash?

    (A) Box 1

    (B) Box 2

    (C) Box 5

    (D) Box 14

24. In which of these boxes would you indicate that Form 3849-D was requested?

    (A) Box 3

    (B) Box 4

    (C) Box 12

    (D) Box 14

25. Which of these would be a correct entry for Box 9?

    (A) John Jones

    (B) 12/2/2008

    (C) #2343

    (D) A checkmark

26. Where would you indicate the date that the payment was sent to the mailer?

    (A) Box 4

    (B) Box 9

    (C) Box 12

    (D) Box 14

27. Which of these would be a correct entry for Box 3?

    (A) A signature

    (B) A checkmark

    (C) A date

    (D) A dollar amount

28. If the customer pays by check, the check must be made payable to which of the following?
    (A) The postal clerk
    (B) The mailer
    (C) The delivery employee
    (D) The United States Postal Service

29. Which of these is a correct entry for Box 8?
    (A) Betty Suarez, 20 Carriage Rd., Trenton, NJ 08618
    (B) Betty Suarez
    (C) 20 Carriage Road
    (D) 08618

30. In which box would you enter the money order number?
    (A) Box 2
    (B) Box 11
    (C) Box 13
    (D) Box 14

ANSWERS TO DRILL: FORMS COMPLETION PRACTICE

1. A	11. C	21. D
2. D	12. B	22. C
3. A	13. D	23. B
4. D	14. D	24. A
5. B	15. A	25. A
6. B	16. B	26. C
7. B	17. D	27. B
8. C	18. A	28. B
9. D	19. A	29. A
10. A	20. D	30. D

Strategies for Improving Your Coding Skills and Your Memory for Addresses

CHAPTER

5

STRATEGIES FOR IMPROVING YOUR CODING SKILLS AND YOUR MEMORY FOR ADDRESSES

5

Part C of the test contains two sections. The coding section contains thirty-six items that must be completed in six minutes. The memory section of Part C is one that will test your memory. You will be given seven minutes to use your memory to match thirty-six number addresses to the appropriate postal code. This may seem like an intimidating section, but early in Part C, Section 1, you will use the same postal codes to assign to a variety of addresses. The difference in the two sections is that in Section 1, the postal codes that you use are printed for your use; in Section 2, you will be required to memorize the address ranges with their assigned codes. With the techniques you will develop in this chapter, you can achieve a high score.

TEST STRATEGIES

Guessing

While completing Part A, Address Checking, of the postal exam, it is suggested that you do not guess because guessing can hurt your score. In Part C, Coding and Memory, guessing does not hurt your score. There-fore, you should make a guess for the problems about which you are not sure. Because there are four answer choices, you have a one in four, or 25 percent, chance of getting the answer correct. You will probably be able to discount one or two choices as not correct by the information you remember, thus making your chances of guessing the correct answer even better.

Because there are four answer choices, you have a one in four, or 25 per-cent, chance of getting the answer correct.

Shortening Information to Memorize

You will be given four boxes to memorize that correspond to delivery routes A, B, C, and D. It is not necessary, however, to memorize all four boxes. If you spend the allotted time memorizing three of the boxes so that you are sure you know the information contained in each, you need not memorize the remaining box. You never actually need to look at the fifth box because it indicates only this: if an address does not fall in one of the address ranges listed for delivery routes A, B, or C, then the answer is delivery route D. When you come across a name, or number and name combination that you do not recognize, you will know that it belongs to the box for delivery route D. This may feel like a bit of a risk because it seems that you are neglecting the information, but this strategy is proven to maximize your time.

Using Every Minute

Prior to beginning this portion of the exam, you will be given three minutes to memorize the address ranges and their corresponding delivery codes in the four boxes. After this memorization period, you will have three minutes to complete sample questions. Some people may find it helpful to complete these questions as a way to gear up for the ones that actually count. Most examinees use this time best, however, by continu-ing to memorize. These three minutes can serve you well in finalizing your memorization process. Because time is allotted for the examiner to check that all test takers clearly understand the directions, you may find that you have a few more minutes to continue memorizing, especially if other test takers have questions.

Techniques for Remembering Numbered Addresses

You will be required to memorize eight sets of numbered addresses.

Association

You may find a personal association with a chunk of numbers. If you can find meaning in combinations of numbers, you may want to form pictures to associate with the characters. For instance, let's say that the first and second lines of numbers, when chunked, make the number 2020. The third line has the number 39. You may say, "In the year 2020, I will be 39 years old." Some associations may be made by dates in history, such as 1492 with Christopher Columbus.

Number Codes

It may take some time to master this form of memorization, but it is proven to be effective. Take time to practice this technique and you will find that it works.

You will need to memorize a letter code for each number from 0 to 9. The letters are assigned by their relationship to the numbers, whether the letter starts with that sound, looks like that letter when written, or has the letter as a middle sound in the word. Memorize the following list.

$$1 = W$$
$$2 = T$$
$$3 = R$$
$$4 = F$$
$$5 = P$$
$$6 = S$$
$$7 = V$$
$$8 = B$$
$$9 = N$$
$$0 = Z$$

In this technique, you will again take the first two numbers of the number address range. Change the numbers to letters. Following are examples of how this would be done.

$$56 = PS$$
$$23 = TR$$
$$71 = VW$$
$$98 = NB$$
$$14 = WF$$

Now you will need to make associations. The number 56 would be PS, which could be made into "pass" by adding a vowel and repeating the last consonant. Vowels may be added between the two consonants. Now match the word with the box in which it is found. This number was found in box A, so a relationship with an "a" word needs to be set up. Perhaps "pass around" would make sense for you. The number 89 would be BN, which could be associated with the word *bin*. If this is in box B, you could say "bread bin." The number 89 is found in box B.

DRILL

Directions: Next to each number, write the letter combination with which it corresponds. Then practice making word associations in the lines next to the letter combinations you have written.

1. 72 _____ _____
2. 53 _____ _____
3. 88 _____ _____
4. 16 _____ _____
5. 92 _____ _____
6. 18 _____ _____
7. 24 _____ _____
8. 36 _____ _____
9. 45 _____ _____
10. 70 _____ _____

ANSWERS

1. 72 = VT
2. 53 = PR
3. 88 = BB
4. 16 = WS
5. 92 = NT

6. 18 = WB
7. 24 = TF
8. 36 = RS
9. 45 = FP
10. 70 = VZ

Here are examples of what you will find in Part C, Section 1, Coding.

DRILL: CODING

Directions: Assign a code to questions 1–36 based on the coding guide below.

CODING GUIDE	
Address Range	**Delivery Route**
1–99 E. State St. 50–599 N. Broad St. 1–299 N. Temple Rd.	A
100–299 E. State St. 300–600 N. Temple Rd.	B
600–800 N. Broad St. 20–100 Center St. 1500–4500 N. Main St.	C
All mail that doesn't fall in one of the address ranges listed above	D

Address	Delivery Route			
1. 23 N. Temple Road	A	B	C	D
2. 355 Elsie Dr.	A	B	C	D
3. 576 N. Broad St.	A	B	C	D
4. 45 Center St.	A	B	C	D
5. 1699 N. Main St.	A	B	C	D

	Address	Delivery Route			
6.	588 N. Broad St.	A	B	C	D
7.	4500 Maine St.	A	B	C	D
8.	29 Centre St., Apt. 345	A	B	C	D
9.	54 Elm St.	A	B	C	D
10.	229 N. Temple Rd.	A	B	C	D
11	85 E. State St.	A	B	C	D
12.	2509 N. Main St.	A	B	C	D
13.	599 N. Brad Street	A	B	C	D
14.	3 N. Temple Rd	A	B	C	D
15	46 Center St.	A	B	C	D
16.	54 E. Elm	A	B	C	D
17.	777 Central	A	B	C	D
18.	555 N. Broad St.	A	B	C	D
19.	55 Charles St.	A	B	C	D
20.	3223 N. Main St., Apt 2-D	A	B	C	D
21.	1 N. Temple Dr.	A	B	C	D
22.	199 E. State St.	A	B	C	D
23.	67 N. Broad St.	A	B	C	D
24.	430 N. Temple Rd.	A	B	C	D
25.	55 Center St.	A	B	C	D
26.	995 N. Broad St.	A	B	C	D
27.	1 Center St.	A	B	C	D
28.	4322 N. Main St.	A	B	C	D
29.	46 Center St.	A	B	C	D
30.	325-23 N. Temple Rd.	A	B	C	D
31.	765 N. Broad St.	A	B	C	D
32.	299 N. Timple Ave.	A	B	C	D
33.	85 Center St.	A	B	C	D
34.	222 E. State St.	A	B	C	D
35.	321 N. Broad St.	A	B	C	D
36.	8D Center St.	A	B	C	D

ANSWERS

1.	A	19.	D
2.	D	20.	C
3.	A	21.	D
4.	C	22.	B
5.	C	23.	A
6.	A	24.	B
7.	D	25.	C
8.	D	26.	D
9.	D	27.	D
10.	A	28.	C
11.	A	29.	C
12.	C	30.	B
13.	D	31.	C
14.	A	32.	D
15.	C	33.	C
16.	D	34.	B
17.	D	35.	A
18.	A	36.	D

Here are examples of what you will find in Part C, Section 2, Memory.

DRILL: MEMORY

Directions: Take three minutes to memorize the coding guide you just used. You should not take any notes while memorizing the guide, but you may write in your test booklet when you answer the items. Move through the following thirty-six questions and assign codes to each based on your memory of the coding guide. Circle the appropriate delivery route code. Do not refer to the guide as you work through this exercise. Work as quickly and as accurately as possible. Time yourself on these examples. You should stop after three minutes. You may not be able to finish them in that amount of time, but if you practice with a time limit, you can get a better sense of the real testing conditions.

	Address		Deliver	y Route	
1.	45 E. State St.	A	B	C	D
2.	67 S. Temple Rd.	A	B	C	D
3.	700 N. Broad St.	A	B	C	D
4.	110 Center St.	A	B	C	D
5.	450 N. Temple Rd.	A	B	C	D
6.	5400 N. Main St.	A	B	C	D
7.	36 Center St.	A	B	C	D
8.	4501 N. Main St.	A	B	C	D
9.	299 Temply Road	A	B	C	D
10.	569 N. Broad St.	A	B	C	D
11.	1500 Main Street	A	B	C	D
12.	299 E. State Rd.	A	B	C	D
13.	645 Broad St.	A	B	C	D
14.	4500-02 N. Main St.	A	B	C	D
15.	22 E. State St.	A	B	C	D
16.	1602 N. Main St., Apt 3-C	A	B	C	D
17.	68 Center St.	A	B	C	D
18.	99 West State St.	A	B	C	D
19.	798 N. Broad St.	A	B	C	D
20.	1500 North Maine Street	A	B	C	D
21.	3 N. Temple Rd.	A	B	C	D
22.	678-C N. Broad St.	A	B	C	D
23.	3500 N. Mains St.	A	B	C	D
24.	475 N. Temple Rd.	A	B	C	D
25.	100 Centre St.	A	B	C	D
26.	43 East State St.	A	B	C	D
27.	200 N. Temple Rd.	A	B	C	D
28.	1670 N. Main St.	A	B	C	D

	Address	Delivery Route			
29.	433 S. Temple Rd.	A	B	C	D
30.	222 E. State St.	A	B	C	D
31.	67D Center St.	A	B	C	D
32.	4500 N. Main St.	A	B	C	D
33.	21 E. State St.	A	B	C	D
34.	54 S. Broad St.	A	B	C	D
35.	1500 S. Main St.	A	B	C	D
36.	2 N. Temple Road	A	B	C	D

ANSWERS

1.	A	19.	C
2.	D	20.	D
3.	C	21.	A
4.	D	22.	C
5.	B	23.	D
6.	D	24.	B
7.	C	25.	D
8.	D	26.	A
9.	D	27.	A
10.	A	28.	C
11.	D	29.	D
12.	D	30.	B
13.	D	31.	C
14.	D	32.	C
15.	A	33.	A
16.	C	34.	D
17.	C	35.	D
18.	D	36.	A

POSTAL EXAMINATION 473/473c

PRACTICE TEST 1

Practice Test 1– 473/473c

PART A: ADDRESS CHECKING

60 Questions
11 Minutes

Directions: Compare the **List to Be Checked** with the **Correct List**. Indicate if (A) there are **No Errors**, (B) there is an error in the **Address Only**, (C) there is an error in the **ZIP Code Only**, or (D) there is an error in **Both** the address and the ZIP code.

A. No Errors	B. Address Only	C. ZIP Code Only	D. Both

Correct List

	Address	ZIP Code
1.	2315 Western Street Tempe, AZ	85281
2.	703 Medaco Road Philadelphia, PA	19101
3.	15 Fischer Place Trenton, NJ	08618
4.	10 Stuyvesant Avenue Trenton, NJ	08618
5.	116 Village Blvd. Princeton, NJ	08540
6.	124-17 Halsey St. Newark, DE	19713

List to Be Checked

Address	ZIP Code
2315 Western Avenue Tempe, AZ	85281
703 Medico Rd. Philadelphia, PA	19101
51 Fisher Place Trenton, NJ	08638
7010 Stuyvesant Ave. Trenton, NJ	08610
116 Village Blvd. Princeton, NJ	08540
124-17 Halsey St. Newark, DE	19173

| A. No Errors | B. Address Only | C. ZIP Code Only | D. Both |

Correct List

	Address	ZIP Code
7.	2300 Atlanta Ave. San Jose, CA	95101
8.	12 Wolfpack Ct. Morristown, NJ	07960
9.	P.O. Box 1343 Pontotoc, MS	38863
10.	3002 Eric Boulevard Syracuse, NY	13202
11.	10-03 Lewis Hwy. Cleveland, OH	44106
12.	650 College Road Moody, AL	35004
13.	1603 S. Broad St. Friendship, AR	71942
14.	812 Executive Drive Vail, CO	81657
15.	20 Armour Way Woody Circle, CO	81656
16.	66 Knapp Ave. Gretna, LA	70054
17.	1670 White Horse-Mercerville Rd. Providence, RI	02940
18.	51 Everett Dr. Trenton, NJ	08618

List to Be Checked

Address	ZIP Code
2300 Altantic Ave. San Jose, CA	95110
12 Wolfpack Ct. Moorestown, NJ	07960
P.O. Box 1343 Pontotoc, MS	38863
3002 Eric Boulevard Syracuse, NY	13222
10-03 Lewis Hwy. Cleveland, OH	44106
605 College Road Moody, AL	35004
1603 N. Broad St. Friendship, AR	79142
8112 Executive Drive Vail, CO	86157
20 Arm Way Woody Circle, CO	81256
66 Knapp Ave. Los Angeles, CA	70054
1670 White Horse-Mercerville Rd. Providence, RI	02940
15 Everett Dr. Trenton, NJ	08168

A. No Errors	B. Address Only	C. ZIP Code Only	D. Both

	Correct List		List to Be Checked	

	Address	ZIP Code	Address	ZIP Code
19.	1239 Parkway Luke, MD	21540	1239 Park Way Luke, MD	21540
20.	4437 State Hwy. Sioux Falls, SD	57103	4437 State Hwy. Sioux Falls, SD	57113
21.	19 Rock Run Dr. Chicago, IL	60616	91 Rocks Run Dr. Chicago, IL	60616
22.	226 Sedona La. Sedona AZ	86339	226 Sedona Lane Rd. Sedona AZ	83369
23.	1735 Wacker Dr. Lake Springs, WI	49456	1735 Wacker Dr. Spring Lake, WI	49456
24.	301 Gentry Road Los Angeles, CA	90013	301 Gentry Road Los Angeles, CA	90013
25.	9423 Mulholland Drive San Diego, CA	92176	9423 Mulholland Drive San Diego, CA	92176
26.	73 Ocean Dr. Henderson, NC	27536	73 Ocean Dr. Hendersonville, NC	28739
27.	8931 Montclair Avenue Portland, OR	50311	8931 Montclair Avenue Portland, ME	04873
28.	2829 Hammond Dr. Hammond, IN	46324	2829 Hammond Dr. Hammond, IN	46234
29.	123 Desert La. Brooklyn, NY	11221	123 Dessert La. Brooklyn, NY	11221
30.	75 Stevenson Ave. Winchendon Springs, MA	01475	75 Stevens Ave. Winchendon Springs, MA	04175

| A. No Errors | B. Address Only | C. ZIP Code Only | D. Both |

Correct List

	Address	ZIP Code
31.	8 Lake Balwin Dr. Flintstone, MD	21530
32.	32 Chambers St. Barclair, MD	21607
33.	1045 Melrose Ave. Vail, CO	81657-1234
34.	701 Kensington Rd East Windsor, NJ	08058
35.	1106 Woodside Pk. Orchard Park, NY	14127
36.	161 Hempstead Rd. Stone Mountain, GA	55791
37.	434 Washington Rd. Butte, MT	59707
38.	1072 Terrace Blvd. Cleveland, OH	44102-1919
39.	1958 Lawrenceville St. Honolulu, HI	96808-9239
40.	348 Grandview Road Kalamazoo, MI	49001
41.	3393 Sunflower Ln. Kings Mountain, NC	28086
42.	2286 Spruce St. Terre Haute, IN	46733

List to Be Checked

Address	ZIP Code
80 Lake Balwin Dr. Flinstone, MD	21530
32 Chambers St. Barclay, MD	21607
1045 Melrose Ave. Vail, CO	81657-1234
701 Kensington Rd West Windsor, NJ	08058
1106 Woodside Park Orchard Park, NY	14127
161 Hempstead Rd. Stone Mountain, GA	55971
334 Washington Rd. Butte, MT	59717
1072 Terrace Blvd. Cleveland, OH	44102-1919
1958 Lawrenceville St. Honolulu, HI	96808-9239
348 Grandview Road Kalamazoo, MI	49100
3393 Sunflower Ln. Kong Mountain, NC	28086
2286 Pine St. Terre Haute, IN	46733

A. No Errors	B. Address Only	C. ZIP Code Only	D. Both

Correct List

	Address	ZIP Code
43.	41-F Chicopee Dr. Miami, FL	33133
44.	233 Wyndham Ln. New York, NY	10004-4782
45.	113 Howsington Pl. Meriden, CT	06450
46.	263-B Middlebury Dr. Decatur, GA	46733
47.	504 Liberty Sq. Broken Arrow, OK	74012
48.	8N Franklin Terrace Lake Stephens, WA	98258
49.	32 Witch's Hollow Wichita, KS	67201
50.	257 Highland Ave. Columbia, SC	29201
51.	32-33 Quail Ridge Dr. San Francisco, CA	94122
52.	265 S. Middlebury Dr. Los Angeles, CA	90016
53.	10 Front St. Valhalla, NY	10595
54.	2427 Sylvan Ave. Grand Rapids, MI	49506

List to Be Checked

Address	ZIP Code
41-F Chicopee Dr. Miami, OK	74354
233 Wyndham Ln. New York, NY	10004-4782
113 Howsington Pl. Honolulu, HI	96088
263-B Middlebury Dr. Decatur, IN	46733
504 Liberty Sq. Broken Arrow, OK	74012
8N Franklin Terrace Stevens Lake, WA	98258
32 Witches Hollow Wichita, KS	67201
257 Highland Ave. Columbia, OH	29201
32-33 Quail Ridge Dr. San Francisco, CO	94222
265 S. Middlebury Dr. Los Angeles, CA	60019
10 Back St. Valhalla, NY	10559
2427 Sylvan Ave. Grand Rapids, MI	49605

A. No Errors	B. Address Only	C. ZIP Code Only	D. Both

	Correct List			**List to Be Checked**	
	Address	*ZIP Code*		*Address*	*ZIP Code*
55.	2301 Garry Rd. Princeton Junction, NJ	08550		2103 Jerry Rd. Princeton Junction, NJ	08550
56.	310 Shady Ln. Jonesboro, AK	72404		310 Shady Ln. Jonesboro, AK	72404
57.	2907 Hunters Glen Dr. Boston, MA	02134		2907 Hunters Dr. Boston, MA	02134
58.	134 Walden Cir. Atlanta, GA	30312		134 Walden Cir. Atlanta, GA	30312
59.	27-317 Blanketflower Ct. New Orleans, LA	70115		317-27 Blanketflower Ct. New Orleans, LA	70111
60.	1603 E. State St. Washington, DC	20503		1603 E. State House St. Washington, DC	20533

PART B: FORMS COMPLETION

30 Questions
15 Minutes

Directions: Read each form and answer the questions based on the information provided.

Questions 1–5 are based on the following information.

AUTHORIZATION TO HOLD MAIL	
NOTE: *Complete and give to your letter carrier or mail to the post office that delivers your mail.*	We can hold your mail for a minimum of **3**, but not for more than **30 days**.

Postmaster: Please hold mail for:

Name(s)	☐ **A.** Please deliver all accumulated mail and resume normal delivery on the ending date shown below.
Address *(Number, street, apt./suite no., city, state, ZIP + 4)*	☐ **B.** I will pick up all accumulated mail when I return and understand that mail delivery will not resume until I do so.

Beginning Date	Ending Date *(May only be changed by the customer in writing)*	Customer Signature

For Post Office Use Only

1. Date Received	
2. Clerk	4. Bin Number
3. Carrier	5. Route Number

(Complete this section only if customer selected option B)

6. ☐ Accumulated mail has been picked up.	7. Resume Delivery of Mail *(Date)*	8. By

1. Where would you enter the carrier's name?
   - (A) Box 2
   - (B) Box 3
   - (C) Box 4
   - (D) Box 6

2. Which of these would be a correct entry for Box 5?
   - (A) Rural Route 202
   - (B) January 10, 2008
   - (C) Michael Lewis
   - (D) A checkmark

3. Which would be a correct entry for Box 1?
   - (A) 3:00 P.M.
   - (B) $5.25
   - (C) 08618
   - (D) 9/2/08

4. In which box would the clerk enter his/her name?
   - (A) Box 2
   - (B) Box 3
   - (C) Box 7
   - (D) Box 8

5. Where would you indicate that the customer has picked up all the mail?
   - (A) Box 1
   - (B) Box 3
   - (C) Box 6
   - (D) Box 8

Questions 6–10 are based on the following information.

INSURED MAIL RECEIPT	
OFFICIAL USE	
1. Postage $	**2a.** ☐ Fragile **2c.** ☐ Perishable **2b.** ☐ Liquid **2d.** ☐ Hazardous
3. Insurance Fee	**4.** Insurance Coverage
5. Restricted Delivery Fee (endorsement required)	**9.** Postmark Here
6. Special Handling Fee	
7. Return Receipt Fee (endorsement required)	
8. Total Postage & Fees $	
10. *Sent to:*	
11. *Street, Apt. No.; or PO Box No.*	
12. *City, State, ZIP + 4* ®	

6. Where would you indicate the postage before applying any fees?
   (A) Box 1
   (B) Box 3
   (C) Box 6
   (D) Box 7

7. In which box would you indicate that the package contains a crystal statuette?
   (A) Box 2a
   (B) Box 2b
   (C) Box 2c
   (D) Box 2d

8. The total paid was $201.86. Where would you indicate this amount?
   (A) Box 3
   (B) Box 4
   (C) Box 8
   (D) Box 10

9. Which would be a correct entry for Box 11?
   (A) Marie Johns
   (B) 11/23/08
   (C) New York, NY 11021
   (D) 31 Greenwich St.

10. A dollar amount would be a correct entry for each box EXCEPT
    (A) Box 1.
    (B) Box 5.
    (C) Box 7.
    (D) Box 9.

Questions 11–18 are based on the following information.

EXPRESS MAIL

Post Office to Addressee

ORIGIN (POSTAL SERVICE USE ONLY)			DELIVERY (POSTAL USE ONLY)			
1. PO ZIP Code	**2.** Day of Delivery ☐ Next ☐ 2nd ☐ 2nd Del. Day	**3.** Postage $	Delivery Attempt Mo. Day	Time	☐ AM ☐ PM	Employee Signature
4. Date Accepted Mo. Day Year	**5.** Scheduled Date of Delivery Month Day	**6.** Return Receipt Fee $	Delivery Attempt Mo. Day	Time	☐ AM ☐ PM	Employee Signature
7. Time Accepted ☐ AM ☐ PM	**8.** Scheduled Time of Delivery ☐ Noon ☐ 3 PM	**9.** COD Fee $	Delivery Date Mo. Day	Time	☐ AM ☐ PM	Employee Signature
		10. Insurance Fee $	**CUSTOMER USE ONLY**			
11. Flat Rate ☐ or Weight lbs. ozs.	**12.** Military ☐ 2nd Day ☐ 3rd Day	**13.** Total Postage & Fees $	**16. PAYMENT BY ACCOUNT** Express Mail Corporate Acct. No.		**17.** Federal Agency Acct. No. or Postal Service Acct. No.	
14. Int'l Alpha Country Code	**15.** Acceptance Emp. Initials					

18. WAIVER OF SIGNATURE *(Domestic Mail Only)*
Additional merchandise insurance is void if customer requests waiver of signature.
I wish delivery to be made without obtaining signature of addressee or addressee's agent (if delivery employee judges that article can be left in secure location) and I authorize that delivery employee's signature constitutes valid proof of delivery.

NO DELIVERY _____
☐ Weekend   Mailer Signature
☐ Holiday

19. FROM: (PLEASE PRINT)   PHONE (   ) _____

20. TO: (PLEASE PRINT)   PHONE (   ) _____

ZIP + 4 (U.S. ADDRESSES ONLY. DO NOT USE FOR FOREIGN POSTAL CODES.)

☐ ☐ ☐ ☐ ☐ **+** ☐ ☐ ☐ ☐

FOR INTERNATIONAL DESTINATIONS, WRITE COUNTRY NAME BELOW.
21.

11. Where on the form would you write the post office's ZIP code?

    (A) Box 1

    (B) Box 14

    (C) Box 18

    (D) Box 20

12. If the letter is being mailed to Paris, France, where would you indicate the country code?

    (A) Box 9

    (B) Box 14

    (C) Box 19

    (D) Box 21

13. In which box is a checkmark plus a signature a correct entry?

    (A) Box 11

    (B) Box 14

    (C) Box 18

    (D) Box 20

14. Which of these would be a correct entry for Box 5?

    (A) August 5

    (B) August 5, 2008

    (C) 8/5

    (D) 8/5/08

15. Which of these would be a correct entry for Box 21?

    (A) Kentucky

    (B) Mr. Harry Jones

    (C) Mexico

    (D) 3121 Main Street, Dallas TX

16. Where would you indicate that the customer has a federal agency account number?

    (A) Box 16

    (B) Box 17

    (C) Box 18

    (D) Box 20

17. Which of these would be a correct entry for Box 20?

    (A) 215-665467

    (B)   08345

    (C) 212-345-7869

    (D) 08536-1919

18. Where would the customer sign a signature waiver?

    (A) Box 18

    (B) Box 19

    (C) Box 20

    (D) Box 21

Questions 19–25 are based on the following information.

CUSTOMS DECLARATION	
Customs Declaration **CN22** May be opened officially See Instructions on Reverse **Do not duplicate without USPS approval.**	**Customs Declaration CN22—Sender's Declaration**
1. ☐ Gift ☐ Commercial sample ☐ Documents ☐ Other	I, the undersigned, whose name and address are given on the item, certify that the particulars given in this declaration are correct and that this item does not contain any dangerous article or articles prohibited by legislation or by postal or customs regulations. This copy will be retained at the post office for 30 days.

1a. Quantity and detailed description of contents	**2.** Weight lb oz	**3.** Value (US $)	**9.** Sender's Name & Address
For commercial items only **4.** *If known,* HS tariff number and **5.** country of origin of goods	**6.** Total Weight	**7.** Total Value (US $)	**10.** Addressee's Name & Address
I, the undersigned, whose name and address are given on the item, certify that the particulars given in this declaration are correct and that this item does not contain any dangerous article or articles prohibited by legislation or by postal or customs regulations.			
8. Date and sender's signature			**11.** Date and sender's signature

19. In which box would you indicate that the package is a gift from the sender?

    (A) Box 1

    (B) Box 1a

    (C) Box 3

    (D) Box 6

20. A customer is mailing a sample of his new product to London. Where would you indicate that the product was produced in China?

    (A) Box 1

    (B) Box 2

    (C) Box 5

    (D) Box 9

21. In which box would the customer enter the address of the person who will receive the package?

    (A) Box 8

    (B) Box 9

    (C) Box 10

    (D) Box 11

22. Which portion of the form is the post office copy?

    (A) Boxes 1 through 8

    (B) Boxes 1 through 3

    (C) Boxes 4 through 8

    (D) Boxes 9 through 11

23. Where would the total weight of 8 lbs., 4 oz. be a correct entry?

    (A) Box 3

    (B) Box 6

    (C) Box 7

    (D) Box 9

24. In which box would "2 men's flannel shirts, 2 pairs of boots" be a correct entry?

    (A) Box 1

    (B) Box 1a

    (C) Box 2

    (D) Box 3

25. The customer's signature would be a correct entry in which box?

    (A) Box 5

    (B) Box 8

    (C) Box 9

    (D) Box 10

Questions 26–30 are based on the following information.

DOMESTIC RETURN RECEIPT	
SENDER: *COMPLETE THIS SECTION*	*COMPLETE THIS SECTION ON DELIVERY*
■ Complete boxes 1, 2, and 3. Also complete box 4 if Restricted Delivery is desired. ■ Print your name and address on the reverse so that we can return the card to you. ■ Attach this card to the back of the mailpiece, or on the front if space permits.	**A.** Signature **X** ☐ Agent ☐ Addressee
1. Article Addressed to:	**B.** Received by *(Printed Name)* **C.** Date of Delivery
	D. Is delivery address different from box 1? If YES, enter delivery address below: ☐ Yes ☐ No

	3. Service Type
	   ☐ Certified Mail ☐ Express Mail
	   ☐ Registered ☐ Return Receipt
	   ☐ Insured Mail for Merchandise
	                     ☐ C.O.D.

2. Article Number *(Transfer from service label)*	**4.** Restricted Delivery? *(Extra Fee)* ☐ Yes

26. If the customer wants restricted delivery, which boxes on the card should he/she complete?

    (A) Boxes 1, 2, and 3 only

    (B) Boxes 2 and 3 only

    (C) Boxes 1, 2, 3, and 4

    (D) Boxes 2, 3, and 4 only

27. Where would the customer print his/her name and address?

    (A) Box 1

    (B) Box 2

    (C) Box 3

    (D) On the back of the card

28. In which box would you indicate that the letter will be sent by registered mail?

    (A) Box 1

    (B) Box 2

    (C) Box 3

    (D) Box 4

29. Which of these would be a correct entry for Box C?

    (A) 4/18/08

    (B) 301 S. Paddock Avenue
        Madison, WI 55301

    (C) James Walker

    (D) 3145-23

30. How would you indicate that the delivery address is different from the one in Box 1?

    (A) Put a checkmark in Box A.

    (B) Put a checkmark in Box D.

    (C) Put a checkmark in Box 3.

    (D) Put a checkmark in Box 4.

PART C: CODING AND MEMORY

Section 1: Coding

36 Questions
6 Minutes

Directions: Assign a code to questions 1–36 based on the coding guide below.

CODING GUIDE	
Address Range	**Delivery Route**
1–99 E. State St. 50–599 N. Broad St. 1–299 N. Temple Rd.	A
100–299 E. State St. 300–600 N. Temple Rd.	B
600–800 N. Broad St. 20–100 Center St. 1500–4500 N. Main St.	C
All mail that doesn't fall in one of the address ranges listed above	D

Address	Delivery Route			
1.	125 E. State St.	A	B	C	D
2.	20 E. State St.	A	B	C	D
3.	2503 N. Main St.	A	B	C	D
4	452 N. Temple Rd.	A	B	C	D
5.	554 N. Broad St.	A	B	C	D
6.	10 Temple Rd.	A	B	C	D
7.	1455 Main St.	A	B	C	D
8.	87 E. State St.	A	B	C	D

	Address	Delivery Route			
9.	10 Center St.	A	B	C	D
10.	708 Broad St.	A	B	C	D
11.	305 S. Temple Rd.	A	B	C	D
12.	30 Center St.	A	B	C	D
13.	80 N. Broad St.	A	B	C	D
14.	300 S. Temple Rd.	A	B	C	D
15.	2500 S. Main St.	A	B	C	D
16.	25 Center St.	A	B	C	D
17.	110 W. State St.	A	B	C	D
18.	3507 N. Main St.	A	B	C	D
19.	605 N. Temple Rd.	A	B	C	D
20.	452 N. Broad St.	A	B	C	D
21.	4500 N. Main St.	A	B	C	D
22.	720 S. Temple Rd.	A	B	C	D
23.	910 N. Broad St.	A	B	C	D
24.	435 N. Temple Rd.	A	B	C	D
25.	97 E. State St.	A	B	C	D
26.	1500 N. Main St.	A	B	C	D
27.	52 Center St.	A	B	C	D
28.	998 N. Broad St.	A	B	C	D
29.	4510 N. Main St.	A	B	C	D
30.	564 S. Temple Rd.	A	B	C	D
31.	24 Center St.	A	B	C	D
32.	200 N. Broad St.	A	B	C	D
33.	700 N. Broad St.	A	B	C	D
34.	44-10 Western Ave.	A	B	C	D
35.	432 N. Broad St.	A	B	C	D
36.	350 N. Temple Rd.	A	B	C	D

Section 2: Memory

36 Questions
7 Minutes

Directions: Take three minutes to memorize the coding guide below. Assign a code based on your memory of the coding guide. This coding guide is the same guide used in the previous coding section.

CODING GUIDE	
Address Range	**Delivery Route**
1–99 E. State St. 50–599 N. Broad St. 1–299 N. Temple Rd.	A
100–299 E. State St. 300–600 N. Temple Rd.	B
600–800 N. Broad St. 20–100 Center St. 1500–4500 N. Main St.	C
All mail that doesn't fall in one of the address ranges listed above	D

	Address	Delivery Route			
1.	3 E. State St.	A	B	C	D
2.	299 N. Temple Rd.	A	B	C	D
3.	600 N. Broad St.	A	B	C	D
4.	205 Center St.	A	B	C	D
5.	110 E. State St.	A	B	C	D
6.	400 N. Temple Rd.	A	B	C	D
7.	4700 N. Main St.	A	B	C	D
8.	200 N. Main St.	A	B	C	D
9.	399 N. Broad St.	A	B	C	D

	Address	Delivery Route			
10.	310 N. Temple Rd.	A	B	C	D
11.	6 Main St.	A	B	C	D
12.	50 Center St.	A	B	C	D
13.	710 N. Broad St.	A	B	C	D
14.	500 N. Temple Rd.	A	B	C	D
15.	550 N. Temple Rd.	A	B	C	D
16.	50 N. Broad St.	A	B	C	D
17.	100 E. State. St.	A	B	C	D
18.	30 Center St.	A	B	C	D
19.	345 N. Main St.	A	B	C	D
20.	1 N. Temple Rd.	A	B	C	D
21.	199 N. Temple Rd.	A	B	C	D
22.	90 Center St.	A	B	C	D
23.	20 Center St.	A	B	C	D
24.	400 N. Temple Rd.	A	B	C	D
25.	2 N. Temple Rd.	A	B	C	D
26.	920 Canary St.	A	B	C	D
27.	5 E. State St.	A	B	C	D
28.	1500 N. Main St.	A	B	C	D
29.	300 N. Temple Rd.	A	B	C	D
30.	50 S. Temple St.	A	B	C	D
31.	40 S. Broad St.	A	B	C	D
32.	76 Center St.	A	B	C	D
33.	199 E. State St.	A	B	C	D
34.	245 N. Temple Rd.	A	B	C	D
35.	100 Center St.	A	B	C	D
36.	3910 E. State St.	A	B	C	D

Practice Test 1– 473/473c

ANSWER KEY

Part A: Address Checking

1.	B	21.	B	41.	B
2.	B	22.	D	42.	B
3.	D	23.	B	43.	D
4.	D	24.	A	44.	A
5.	A	25.	A	45.	D
6.	C	26.	D	46.	B
7.	D	27.	D	47.	A
8.	B	28.	C	48.	B
9.	A	29.	B	49.	B
10.	C	30.	D	50.	B
11.	A	31.	B	51.	D
12.	C	32.	B	52.	C
13.	D	33.	A	53.	D
14.	D	34.	B	54.	C
15.	D	35.	B	55.	B
16.	B	36.	C	56.	A
17.	A	37.	D	57.	B
18.	D	38.	A	58.	A
19.	B	39.	A	59.	D
20.	C	40.	C	60.	D

Part B: Forms Completion

1.	B	11.	A	21.	C
2.	A	12.	B	22.	D
3.	D	13.	C	23.	B
4.	A	14.	A	24.	B
5.	C	15.	C	25.	B
6.	A	16.	B	26.	C
7.	A	17.	D	27.	D
8.	C	18.	A	28.	C
9.	D	19.	A	29.	A
10.	D	20.	C	30.	B

Part C: Coding and Memory

Section 1: Coding

1.	B	13.	A	25.	A
2.	A	14.	D	26.	C
3.	C	15.	D	27.	C
4.	B	16.	C	28.	D
5.	A	17.	D	29.	D
6.	D	18.	C	30.	D
7.	D	19.	D	31.	C
8.	A	20.	A	32.	A
9.	D	21.	C	33.	C
10.	D	22.	D	34.	D
11.	D	23.	D	35.	A
12.	C	24.	B	36.	B

Section 2: Memory

1.	A	13.	C	25.	A
2.	A	14.	B	26.	D
3.	C	15.	B	27.	A
4.	D	16.	A	28.	C
5.	B	17.	B	29.	B
6.	B	18.	C	30.	D
7.	D	19.	D	31.	D
8.	D	20.	A	32.	C
9.	A	21.	A	33.	B
10.	B	22.	C	34.	A
11.	D	23.	C	35.	C
12.	C	24.	B	36.	D

POSTAL EXAMINATION 473/473c

PRACTICE TEST 2

Practice Test 2– 473/473c

PART A: ADDRESS CHECKING

60 Questions
11 Minutes

Directions: Compare the **List to Be Checked** with the **Correct List**. Indicate if (A) there are **No Errors**, (B) there is an error in the **Address Only**, (C) there is an error in the **ZIP Code Only**, or (D) there is an error in **Both** the address and the ZIP code.

| A. No Errors | B. Address Only | C. ZIP Code Only | D. Both |

Correct List

	Address	ZIP Code
1.	2332 New Garden Dr. Greensboro, NC	27410
2.	217 Peyton Woods Tr. SW Atlanta, GA	30311
3.	803 Carrington Ave. Seat Pleasant, MD	20743
4.	1617 Greenmeadow Way Largo, MD	20772
5.	753 Mesa College Dr. San Diego, CA	92111
6.	6348 Seastone Way Sacramento, CA	95831

List to Be Checked

Address	ZIP Code
2332 New Garden Dr. Greensboro, NC	27410
217 Peyton Tr. SW Atlanta, GA	30311
803 Carrington Ave. Seat Pleasant, MD	20473
1617 Greenmeadow Way Largo, MD	20772
753 College Dr. San Diego, CA	91111
6348 Seastone Way Sacramento, CA	98531

A. No Errors	B. Address Only	C. ZIP Code Only	D. Both

| **Correct List** | | **List to Be Checked** | |

	Address	ZIP Code	Address	ZIP Code
7.	3009 LaSalle St. Nashville, TN	32709	3009 LaSally St. Nashville, TN	32709
8.	1522 Oak St. Columbia, SC	29204	1522 Oak St. Columbia, NC	29240
9.	206 Parrish Ave. Newport News, VA	23607	206 Parrish Ave. Newport News, VA	23607
10.	4101 15th St. NE Seattle, WA	98195	4101 15th St. NE Seattle, WA	89195
11.	35 Chestley Dr. Macon, GA	31201	35 Chestnut Dr. Macon, GA	31201
12.	8251 Ellery Dr. Dallas, TX	75243	8251 Ellery Dr. Houston, TX	75543
13.	9 Cameron St. Detroit, MI	48203	9 Cameron St. Detroit, MI	48203
14.	77 Lozier St. Rochester, NY	14611	77 Lozier St. Rochester, NY	14611
15.	5741 Jardin Pl. Columbus, OH	43213	5741 Garden Pl. Columbus, OH	43213
16.	6193-W Robin Run Indianapolis, IN	46254	6193-S Robin Run Indianapolis, MN	46254
17.	1405 Nicholson St. Hyattsville, MD	20782	1405 Nicholson St. Hyattsville, MD	20082
18.	465 Washington Ave. #2H Brooklyn, NY	11238	465 Washington Ave. #2H Brooklyn, NY	11238

| A. No Errors | B. Address Only | C. ZIP Code Only | D. Both |

Correct List

List to Be Checked

	Address	ZIP Code	Address	ZIP Code
19.	614 W. 157th St. New York, NY	10032	614 W. 157th St. New York, NY	10002
20.	968 Laurel Ave. Bridgeport, CT	06604	968 S. Laurel Ave. Bridgeport, CT	16642
21.	1450 Terry Ave. Detroit, MI	48235	1450 Merry Ave. Detroit, MI	48235
22.	4400 Lindell Blvd. St. Louis, MO	63108	4400 Lindell Blvd. St. Louis, MO	83108
23.	9771 Goodluck Rd. Gary, IN	46403	9771 Goodluck Rd. Gary, IN	46403
24.	779 Saddle River Rd. Monsey, NY	10952	779 Saddle Lake Rd. Monsey, NY	90152
25.	2 Penn Circle St. Philadelphia, PA	19101	2 Penn Circle St. Philadelphia, PA	91091
26.	912 S. Parnell St. Chicago, IL	60620	912 S. Parnell St. Chicago, IL	60602
27.	701 Park Ave. Minneapolis, MN	55417	701 Park Ave. Minneapolis, MN	55417
28.	7212 Pepper Tree Ln. Long Beach, CA	90815	7212 Pepper Mill Ln. Long Beach, CA	90815
29.	3403 Spruce St. Inkster, MI	48141	3403 Spruce St. Inkster, MI	48141
30.	3639 Liberty Heights Ave. Baltimore, MD	21215	3639 Liberty Eights Ave. Baltimore, MD	21255

| A. No Errors | B. Address Only | C. ZIP Code Only | D. Both |

	Correct List			**List to Be Checked**	
	Address	*ZIP Code*		*Address*	*ZIP Code*
31.	641 New St. White Plains, NY	10604		641 Newland St. White Plains, NY	10604
32.	9910 Royal Ln. Dallas, TX	75231		9910 King Rd. Dallas, TX	72511
33.	P.O. Box 231 Bristol, TN	37621		P.O. Box 231 Bristol, TN	37621
34.	1106 Overmoor St. Oakland, CA	94605		1106 Overmore St. Oakland, CA	94605
35.	2641 Rankin Mill Rd. Denver, CO	80239		2641 Randall Mill Rd. Denver, CO	80239
36.	1700 Broadway, Suite 2400 Chicago, IL	60602- 2504		1700 Broadway Rd., Suite 2400 Chicago, IL	60602- 2504
37.	205 Haviland Dr. Florence, AL	35630		205 Haviland Dr. Florence, AL	25630
38.	39321 NW 63rd St. Miami, FL	33150		39321 NW 63rd St. Tampa, FL	33333
39.	125 Elmhurst Ave. Bristol, PA	19007		125 Elmhurst Ave. Bristol, PA	19007
40.	2211 Creekside Ct. Lawrenceville, NJ	08648		112 Creekside Ct. Lawrenceville, NJ	08648
41.	340-25 Deer Run Ln. Waterbury, CT	06705		340-25 Deer Run Ln. Waterbury, MT	06750
42.	4395 Simon St. Metarie, LA	70003		4395 Simon St. New Orleans, LA	70003

A. No Errors	B. Address Only	C. ZIP Code Only	D. Both

Correct List

	Address	ZIP Code
43.	641-23 145th St. New York, NY	10031
44.	1011 W. 3rd St. Yellow Springs, OH	45387
45.	9221 Buttonwood St. Reading, PA	19604
46.	4021 SW 6th Way Deerfield Beach, FL	33441
47.	Six Pear Tree Ct. Greensboro, NC	27401
48.	36 John St. Amherst, NY	14228
49.	34 Paul Revere Ct. Beaufort, SC	29901
50.	1200 E. Washington Ln. Kannapolis, NC	29081
51.	1500 Seemore Dr. Harrisburg, PA	17111
52.	621 SW 76 St. Kendall, FL	33173
53.	110 Front St. Plainsboro, NJ	08536
54.	6489 Newport Rd Hightstown, NJ	08512

List to Be Checked

Address	ZIP Code
641-23 145th St. New York, NY	13331
1011 W. 3rd St. New Springs, OH	45387
9221 Buttonwood St. Reading, PA	19604
4021 SW 6th Way Deerfield Beach, FL	33441
Six Plum Tree Ct. Greensboro, NC	27401
36 John St. Amherst, NJ	08228
34 Paul Revere Ct. Beaufort, SC	29999
1200 E. Washington Ln. Kannapolis, NC	29081
1500 Seamoore Dr. Harrisburg, PA	17111
621 NW 66 St. Kendall, FL	33773
110 Front St. Plainsboro, NJ	08536
6489 Carport Rd Hightstown, NJ	08512

A. No Errors	B. Address Only	C. ZIP Code Only	D. Both

	Correct List			**List to Be Checked**	
	Address	*ZIP Code*		*Address*	*ZIP Code*
55.	2301 Garry Rd. Philadelphia, PA	19139		2301 Garry Rd. Pittsburgh, PA	19319
56.	13 Ridgewood Ave. Cleveland, OH	44128		13 Ridgewood Ave. Cleveland, OH	14128
57.	5997 Glen Eagles Dr. W. Bloomfield, MI	48323		5997 Glen Eagles Dr. W. Bloomfield, MI	48323
58.	201 1st Ave. N. Vallejo, CA	9491		20 1st Ave. N. Vallejo, CA	9491
59.	1700 Broadway New York, NY	10019		1700 Broadway New York, NY	10919
60.	3 Maureen Drive Burlington, MA	01803-5961		3 Maureen Drive Burlingame, MA	01803-5661

PART B: FORMS COMPLETION

30 Questions
15 Minutes

Directions: Read each form and answer the questions based on the information provided.

Questions 1–5 are based on the following information.

AIRMAIL RECEIPT FOR INTERNATIONAL MAIL							
Completed by the office of origin.	Item Description	1. ☐ Registered Article	2. ☐ Letter	3. ☐ Printed Matter	4. ☐ Other	5. ☐ Recorded Delivery	6. ☐ Express Mail International
	7. Insured Parcel		8. Insured Value			9. Article Number	
	10. Office of Mailing					11. Date of Posting	
	12. Addressee Name or Firm						
	13. Street and No.						
	14. Place and Country						
Completed at destination.	This receipt must be signed by, (1) the addressee; or, (2) a person authorized to sign under the regulations of the country of destination; or, (3) if those regulations so provide, by the employee of the office of destination. This signed form will be returned to the sender by the first mail.						
	15. ☐ The article mentioned above was duly delivered.		16. Date			19. Postmark of the office of destination	
	17. Signature of Addressee		18. Office of Destination Employee Signature				

1. Where would you indicate that the item is a letter?
   (A) Box 1
   (B) Box 2
   (C) Box 3
   (D) Box 4

2. Where would you enter the name of the post office of origin?
   (A) Box 9
   (B) Box 10
   (C) Box 13
   (D) Box 14

3. Which would be a correct entry for Box 14?
   (A) Hamburg, Germany
   (B) June 4, 2008
   (C) $50.00
   (D) Piscataway, New Jersey

4. In which box would the clerk stamp the postmark of the office of destination?

    (A) Box 7

    (B) Box 11

    (C) Box 16

    (D) Box 19

5. Where would you indicate that the letter was delivered?

    (A) Boxes 1 and 13

    (B) Boxes 10 and 12

    (C) Boxes 5 and 15

    (D) Boxes 11 and 14

Questions 6–10 are based on the following information.

RECEIPT FOR REGISTERED MAIL	
1. Registered No.	**8.** Date Stamp
To Be Completed By Post Office	
2. Reg. Fee	
3. Handling Charge	**4.** Return Receipt
5. Postage	**6.** Restricted Delivery
7. Received by	
9. Customer Must Declare Full Value $	Domestic Insurance up to $25,000 is included based upon the declared value. International Indemnity is limited. (See Reverse).
OFFICIAL USE	
To Be Completed by Customer (Please Print) All Entries Must Be In Ballpoint or Typed	
10. FROM	
11. TO	

6. Where would you indicate the postage before applying any fees?
   (A) Box 1
   (B) Box 2
   (C) Box 4
   (D) Box 5

7. Where would you indicate receipt of the registered item?
   (A) Box 1
   (B) Box 4
   (C) Box 7
   (D) Box 9

8. Where would you indicate that the total postage is $10.00?
   (A) Box 2
   (B) Box 3
   (C) Box 5
   (D) Box 9

9. Which would be a correct entry for Box 8?
   (A) Tom Smith
   (B) 501 Center St., New York
   (C) Yes
   (D) Post office date stamp

10. A dollar amount would be a correct entry for each box EXCEPT
    (A) Box 1
    (B) Box 2
    (C) Box 3
    (D) Box 5

Questions 11–16 are based on the following information.

DELIVERY CONFIRMATION RECEIPT
Postage and Delivery Confirmation fees must be paid before mailing
1. *DELIVERY CONFIRMATION NUMBER:*   0308   0070   0000   9193   5883
2. Article Sent To: (to be completed by mailer)

3. Postmark Here	**4.** POSTAL CUSTOMER: Keep this receipt. For inquiries Access internet web site or call 1-800-000-0000
	5. CHECK ONE (POSTAL USE ONLY) ☐ Priority Mail™ Service ☐ First-Class Mail® parcel ☐ Package Services parcel

11. Where on the form would you find the delivery confirmation number?

(A) Box 1

(B) Box 3

(C) Box 4

(D) Box 5

12. If the customer has questions about the delivery of his/her letter, what should he/she do?

(A) Ask his/her letter carrier

(B) Go to the USPS website

(C) Call the Postmaster General

(D) Refuse to pay the delivery confirmation fees

13. In which box is a checkmark a correct entry?

    (A) Box 1

    (B) Box 2

    (C) Box 3

    (D) Box 5

14. According to the form, which of the following is NOT true?

    (A) The customer should keep the receipt.

    (B) Postage and delivery confirmation fees must be paid before mailing.

    (C) The letter carrier must enter the address to which the article is going to be mailed.

    (D) Priority Mail, First-Class Mail parcel, or Package Services parcel must be checked.

15. Which of these would be a correct entry for Box 3?

    (A) 0308 0070 0000 9193 5883

    (B) Post office postmark

    (C) 1-800-22201811

    (D) Matthew Jones
        23 Princeton Ave.
        Princeton, NJ 08540

16. Where would you indicate that the customer wishes to use Priority Mail?

    (A) Box 2

    (B) Box 3

    (C) Box 4

    (D) Box 5

Questions 17–23 are based on the following information.

RETURN RECEIPT FOR MERCHANDISE	
(Domestic Mail Only; No Insurance Coverage Provided)	
8002 1040 0006 6807 7832	
1. ☐ WAIVER OF SIGNATURE I wish delivery to be made without obtaining signature of the addressee or the addressee's agent. I authorize the delivery employee to sign that the shipment was delivered and understand that the signature of the delivery employee will constitute valid proof of delivery. (CUSTOMER SIGNATURE)	
2. 8002 1040 0006 6807 7832	
3. Postage $	**8.** Postmark Here
4. Return Receipt for Merchandise Fee (Endorsement Required)	
5. Special Handling Fee	
6. Total Postage & Fees $	
7. Waiver of Signature ☐ YES ☐ NO	
9. *Sent To*	
10. *Street, Apt. No.; or PO Box No.*	
11. *City, State, ZIP+4*	

17. Which of these would be a correct entry for Box 3?

    (A) $5.65

    (B) Yes

    (C) P.O. Box 2

    (D) Mary Smith

18. Where would the customer check that she is waiving the signature request?

    (A) Box 2

    (B) Box 4

    (C) Box 6

    (D) Box 7

19. In which box would you indicate that the customer is paying a special handling fee?

    (A) Box 3

    (B) Box 5

    (C) Box 6

    (D) Box 7

20. Which box should be completed if the item is being mailed to England?

    (A) Box 9

    (B) Box 10

    (C) Box 11

    (D) This form should not be used.

21. Fees can be entered in all of the boxes EXCEPT

    (A) Box 3.

    (B) Box 4.

    (C) Box 5.

    (D) Box 6.

22. In which box would you check that insurance coverage is provided?

    (A) Box 8

    (B) Box 9

    (C) Box 10

    (D) No insurance coverage is provided.

23. In which box would the customer sign a signature waiver?
    (A) Box 1
    (B) Box 7
    (C) Box 8
    (D) Box 9

Questions 24–30 are based on the following information.

CERTIFIED MAIL RECEIPT	
(Domestic Mail Only; No Insurance Coverage Provided)	
1. Postage $	**6.** Postmark Here
2. Certified Fee	
3. Return Receipt Fee (Endorsement Required)	
4. Restricted Delivery Fee (Endorsement Required)	
5. Total Postage & Fees $	
7. *Sent To*	
8. *Street, Apt. No.; or PO Box No.*	
9. *City, State, ZIP+4®*	

24. Which would be a correct entry for Box 7?

    (A) Vernon Walker

    (B) $200

    (C) 25 Main St.

    (D) Tucson, AZ

25. Where would you indicate the total postage?

    (A) Box 2

    (B) Box 3

    (C) Box 4

    (D) Box 5

26. Which box would be completed if the customer wants restricted delivery?

    (A) Box 2

    (B) Box 3

    (C) Box 4

    (D) Box 6

27. Where would the customer indicate that the box will be sent to Athens, Georgia?

    (A) Box 2

    (B) Box 7

    (C) Box 8

    (D) Box 9

28. In which box would you stamp the postmark on the receipt?

    (A) Box 3

    (B) Box 4

    (C) Box 5

    (D) Box 6

29. Which of these would be a correct entry for Box 2?

    (A) Gina Ross

    (B) P.O. Box 45

    (C) $6.95

    (D) No

30. How would you indicate that the customer wants a return receipt?

    (A) Put a checkmark in Box 3 and fill out a return receipt form.

    (B) Put a checkmark in Box 4 and sign the form.

    (C) Put a checkmark in Box 6.

    (D) Put a checkmark in Box 8.

 PART C: CODING AND MEMORY

Section 1: Coding

36 Questions
6 Minutes

Directions: Assign a code to questions 1–36 based on the coding guide below.

CODING GUIDE	
Address Range	**Delivery Route**
10–99 S. Main St. 220–580 Elsie Dr. 100–499 Paddock Rd.	A
200–359 S. Main St. 500–700 Paddock Rd.	B
581–600 Elsie Dr. 2–100 Rock Run Dr. 1250–2500 Mountain Ln.	C
All mail that doesn't fall in one of the address ranges listed above	D

	Address	Delivery Route			
1.	25 S. Main St.	A	B	C	D
2.	299 S. Main St.	A	B	C	D
3.	600 Elsie Dr.	A	B	C	D
4.	1300 Mountain Ln.	A	B	C	D
5.	122 Paddock Rd.	A	B	C	D
6.	98 Rock Run Dr.	A	B	C	D
7.	2500 Rock Mountain Ln.	A	B	C	D
8.	781 Elsie Dr.	A	B	C	D
9.	500 Elsie Dr.	A	B	C	D
10.	643 Paddock Rd.	A	B	C	D
11.	360 S. Main St.	A	B	C	D
12.	1290-C Mountain Ln.	A	B	C	D
13.	300 Elsie Dr.	A	B	C	D
14.	692 Paddock Rd.	A	B	C	D
15.	282-A Paddock Rd.	A	B	C	D
16.	199 E. Main St.	A	B	C	D
17.	98 Rock Run Dr.	A	B	C	D
18.	342 Paddock Rd.	A	B	C	D
19.	25 S. Main St.	A	B	C	D
20.	622 Paddock Rd.	A	B	C	D
21.	310 Elsie Dr.	A	B	C	D
22.	22 Rock Run Dr.	A	B	C	D
23.	1250 Mountain View Dr.	A	B	C	D
24.	632 Paddock Rd.	A	B	C	D
25.	599 Elsie Dr.	A	B	C	D
26.	299 Elsie Dr.	A	B	C	D
27.	101 Rock Run Dr.	A	B	C	D
28.	2101 Mountain Ln.	A	B	C	D
29.	433 Elsie Dr.	A	B	C	D
30.	201 S. Main St.	A	B	C	D

	Address	Delivery Route			
31.	101 S. Main St.	A	B	C	D
32.	178 Paddock Rd.	A	B	C	D
33.	493 S. Main St.	A	B	C	D
34.	29 Rock Run Dr.	A	B	C	D
35.	663 Paddock Rd.	A	B	C	D
36.	580 S. Elsie Dr.	A	B	C	D

Section 2: Memory

36 Questions
7 Minutes

Directions: Take three minutes to memorize the coding guide below. Assign a code based on your memory of the coding guide. This coding guide is the same guide used in the previous coding section.

CODING GUIDE	
Address Range	**Delivery Route**
10–99 S. Main St. 220–580 Elsie Dr. 100–499 Paddock Rd.	A
200–359 S. Main St. 500–700 Paddock Rd.	B
581–600 Elsie Dr. 2–100 Rock Run Dr. 1250–2500 Mountain Ln.	C
All mail that doesn't fall in one of the address ranges listed above	D

	Address	Delivery Route			
1.	33 S. Main St.	A	B	C	D
2.	582 Elsie Dr.	A	B	C	D
3.	500 Paddock Rd.	A	B	C	D
4.	4400 Mountain Ln.	A	B	C	D
5.	359 S. Main St.	A	B	C	D
6.	2 Rock Run Dr.	A	B	C	D
7.	199 S. Main St.	A	B	C	D
8.	600 N. Elsie Dr.	A	B	C	D
9.	44 Rock Run Dr.	A	B	C	D
10.	1259 Mountain Ln.	A	B	C	D
11	299 S. Main St.	A	B	C	D
12.	377 Paddock Rd.	A	B	C	D
13.	300 S. Main St.	A	B	C	D
14.	2000 Mountain Ln.	A	B	C	D
15.	632 N. Main St.	A	B	C	D
16.	199 N. Main St.	A	B	C	D
17.	99 Rock Run Dr.	A	B	C	D
18.	500 Elsie Dr.	A	B	C	D
19.	125 Paddock Rd.	A	B	C	D
20.	342 S. Main St.	A	B	C	D
21.	301 Elsie Dr.	A	B	C	D
22.	21 Rock Run Dr.	A	B	C	D
23.	1251 Mountain View Dr.	A	B	C	D
24.	664 Paddock Rd.	A	B	C	D
25.	596 Elsie Dr.	A	B	C	D
26.	280 Elsie Dr.	A	B	C	D
27.	111 Rock Run Dr.	A	B	C	D
28.	2222 Mountain Ln.	A	B	C	D
29.	423 Elsie Dr.	A	B	C	D
30.	222 S. Main St.	A	B	C	D

	Address	Delivery Route			
31.	111 S. Main St.	A	B	C	D
32.	187 Paddock Rd.	A	B	C	D
33.	495 S. Main St.	A	B	C	D
34.	27 Rock Run Dr.	A	B	C	D
35.	665 Paddock Rd.	A	B	C	D
36.	590 Center St.	A	B	C	D

Practice Test 2 – 473/473c

ANSWER KEY

Part A: Address Checking

1. A	21. B	41. D
2. B	22. C	42. C
3. C	23. A	43. C
4. A	24. D	44. B
5. D	25. C	45. A
6. C	26. C	46. A
7. B	27. A	47. B
8. D	28. B	48. D
9. A	29. A	49. C
10. C	30. D	50. A
11. B	31. B	51. B
12. D	32. D	52. D
13. A	33. A	53. A
14. A	34. B	54. B
15. B	35. B	55. D
16. B	36. B	56. C
17. C	37. C	57. A
18. A	38. D	58. B
19. C	39. A	59. C
20. D	40. B	60. D

Part B: Forms Completion

1. B	11. A	21. B
2. B	12. B	22. D
3. A	13. D	23. A
4. D	14. C	24. A
5. C	15. B	25. D
6. B	16. D	26. C
7. C	17. A	27. D
8. C	18. D	28. D
9. D	19. B	29. C
10. A	20. D	30. A

Part C: Coding and Memory

Section 1: Coding

1. A	13. A	25. C
2. B	14. B	26. A
3. C	15. A	27. D
4. C	16. D	28. C
5. A	17. C	29. A
6. C	18. A	30. B
7. D	19. A	31. D
8. D	20. B	32. A
9. A	21. A	33. D
10. B	22. C	34. C
11. D	23. D	35. B
12. C	24. B	36. D

Section 2: Memory

1.	A	13.	B	25.	C
2.	C	14.	C	26.	A
3.	B	15.	D	27.	D
4.	D	16.	D	28.	C
5.	B	17.	C	29.	A
6.	C	18.	A	30.	B
7.	D	19.	A	31.	D
8.	D	20.	B	32.	A
9.	C	21.	A	33.	D
10.	C	22.	C	34.	C
11.	B	23.	D	35.	B
12.	A	24.	B	36.	D

POSTAL EXAMINATION 473/473c

PRACTICE TEST 3

Practice Test 3– 473/473c

 PART A: ADDRESS CHECKING

60 Questions
11 Minutes

Directions: Compare the **List to Be Checked** with the **Correct List**. Indicate if (A) there are **No Errors**, (B) there is an error in the **Address Only**, (C) there is an error in the **ZIP Code Only**, or (D) there is an error in **Both** the address and the ZIP code.

A. No Errors	B. Address Only	C. ZIP Code Only	D. Both

<table>
<tr><th colspan="3">Correct List</th><th colspan="3">List to Be Checked</th></tr>
<tr><th></th><th>Address</th><th>ZIP Code</th><th></th><th>Address</th><th>ZIP Code</th></tr>
<tr><td>1.</td><td>29 Hamburg Ave. Winterthur, DE</td><td>19735</td><td></td><td>29 Hamburg Ave. Winterthur, DE</td><td>17935</td></tr>
<tr><td>2.</td><td>240 So. Prince Blvd. Portland, ME</td><td>04101</td><td></td><td>240 So. Prince Blvd. Portland, ME</td><td>04101</td></tr>
<tr><td>3.</td><td>22-A Varrick St. New York, NY</td><td>10016</td><td></td><td>22-A Varik St. New York, NY</td><td>10016</td></tr>
<tr><td>4.</td><td>2501 W. Huston Lane Birmingham, AL</td><td>35202</td><td></td><td>2501 W. Huston Lane Birmingham, AL</td><td>35002</td></tr>
<tr><td>5.</td><td>2C November Rd. Old Saybrook, CT</td><td>06475</td><td></td><td>2C November Rd. Old Brooksay, CT</td><td>06475</td></tr>
<tr><td>6.</td><td>460 Highway 66 Houston, TX</td><td>77006</td><td></td><td>461 Highway 66 Houston, TX</td><td>77006</td></tr>
</table>

| A. No Errors | B. Address Only | C. ZIP Code Only | D. Both |

Correct List

	Address	ZIP Code
7.	35 No. 5th Ave. Indianapolis, IN	46220
8.	412A Spring Lane Middletown, CT	06457
9.	2121 Broadway Moorhead, ND	56560
10.	232d Blake Ave. Little Rock, AR	72202
11.	247 Church Blvd., Ste. 22 Atlanta, GA	30309
12.	29 Roanoke Lane Princeton, NJ	08540
13.	4113E No. Campus Rd. Minneapolis, MN	55403-2477
14.	14 Florence Court Oklahoma City, OK	73102
15.	46D Grandview Place Norfolk, VA	23510
16.	46 Liberty Drive Pittsburgh, PA	15223
17.	51 Mott Place Tacoma, WA	98402
18.	65 Mulberry Lane La Jolla, CA	92037

List to Be Checked

Address	ZIP Code
35 So. 5th Ave. Indianapolis, IN	46220
412A Spring Lane Middletown, CT	06457
2121 Broad Way Moorhead, ND	56560
232d Blake Ave. Little Rock, AR	72202
247 Church Rd., Ste. 22 Atlanta, GA	30309
29 Roanoke Lane Princeton, NJ	08540
4113N No. Campus Rd. Minneapolis, MN	55403-2744
41 Florence Court Oklahoma City, OK	73102
46B Grandview Place Norfolk, VA	23510
46 Liberty Drive Pittsburgh, PA	15223
51 Mott Place Tacoma, WA	98402
65 Mulberry Ave. La Jolla, CA	90237

A. No Errors	B. Address Only	C. ZIP Code Only	D. Both

	Correct List			List to Be Checked	
	Address	*ZIP Code*		*Address*	*ZIP Code*
19.	2156 Stanley Ave. Boston, MA	02130		2561 Stanley Ave. Boston, MA	02130
20.	47D Channing Way Eau Claire, WI	54702-4004		47D Channing Way Eau Claire, WI	54702-4004
21.	2C Grant Rd. Elmhurst, IL	60126		2K Grant Rd. Elmhurst, IL	60126
22.	622 Gable Court New Orleans, LA	70124		622 Grable Court New Orleans, LA	70124
23.	12 Cooper St. Washington, DC	20018		12 Cooper St. Washington, DC	20081
24.	7F McCrae Way San Antonio, TX	78202		7F MacCrea Way San Antonio, TX	78202
25.	47R Lugosi St. Palmyra, NJ	08065		47R Lugozi St. Palmyra, NJ	08065
26.	46F Turner Ave. Allison Park, PA	15101		46F Turner Ave. Allison Park, PA	15101
27.	902 Randall Drive New York, NY	10012		209 Randall Drive New York, NY	10012
28.	10510 Hutton Place Greenville, SC	29607		10510 Hutton Place Greenville, SC	29706
29.	55 Quinn St. Sandpoint, ID	83864		55 Quinn St. Sandpoint, ID	83864
30.	362 Davis Road Hollywood, CA	90028		362 Davies Road Hollywood, CA	90028

A. No Errors	B. Address Only	C. ZIP Code Only	D. Both

Correct List		**List to Be Checked**	

	Address	ZIP Code	Address	ZIP Code
31.	15 Andress-Russell Lane Newark, NJ	07102	15 Andress-Russell Lane Newark, NJ	07201
32.	23 Hepburn Ave. Wisconsin Rapids, WI	54494	23 Hepburn Ave. Wisconsin Rapids, WI	54494
33.	206A Reeves Ave. Kansas City, MO	64111	206D Reeves Ave. Kansas City, MO	46111
34.	311-4c Plymouth Lane Los Angeles, CA	90043	311-4c Plymouth Lane Los Angeles, GA	90043
35.	4D Merrill Ave. Chicago, IL	60602	4D Merrill Ave. Chicago, IL	60602
36.	114 Winding Forest Blvd. Amherst, MA	01003-3910	141 Winding Forest Blvd. Amherst, MA	01003-3910
37.	1156 Huron St. Hillside, NJ	07205	1165 Huron St. Hillside, NJ	07250
38.	721 US Hwy. 19 Fresno, CA	93710	127 US Hwy. 19 Fresno, CA	97310
39.	58 Lake Ave. Durham, NC	27707	58 Lake Ave. Durham, NC	27707
40.	75 No. Wilding Ave. Vero Beach, FL	32963	75 No. Wilding Ave. Vero Beach, FL	32963
41.	6511 Delores St. Flushing, NY	11354	6511 Delores St. Flushing, NY	11435
42.	1078 Veronica Ave. Philadelphia, PA	19102	1078 Veronica Place Philadelphia, PA	91202

| A. No Errors | B. Address Only | C. ZIP Code Only | D. Both |

Correct List

	Address	ZIP Code
43.	2125D Paul Blvd. Hilton Head, SC	29926
44.	3537 US Hwy. 22 Durham, NC	27701
45.	38 Rosewood St. Carrollton, TX	75006
46.	56D Woodland Rd. Greenville, MS	38701
47.	1847 No. Carter Ave. Santa Monica, CA	90405
48.	439S Byron Place Flagstaff, AZ	86001
49.	8R West Dunne Court Bethlehem, PA	18018
50.	19 Sixth St. Orlando, FL	32801
51.	1H Westminster Rd. Latham, NY	12110
52.	2030 US Hwy. 11 Arlington, VA	22201
53.	115 Park Gate St. Phoenix, AZ	85014
54.	35 Cloister Court Cherry Hill, NJ	08034

List to Be Checked

Address	ZIP Code
2125D Paulus Blvd. Hilton Head, SC	29996
3573 US Hwy. 22 Durham, NC	21707
38 Rosewood St. Carrollton, TX	75006
56D Woodland Rd. Greenville, MS	83107
1847 No. Carter St. Saint Monica, CA	90405
439S Byron Place Flagstaff, AZ	86001
8R West Dun Court Bethlehem, PA	18018
19 Sixth Ave. Orlando, FL	32108
1K Westminster Rd. Lathem, NY	12111
2011 US Hwy. 30 Arlington, VA	22201
115 Park Gate St. Phoenix, AZ	85114
35 Closster Court Cherry Hill, NJ	08034

A. No Errors	B. Address Only	C. ZIP Code Only	D. Both

Correct List

	Address	ZIP Code
55.	2765 Avenelle Ave. Corning, NY	14830
56.	2131B Winding Hill Lane Canton, OH	44720-7599
57.	65 Brando Terrace Carlisle, PA	17013
58.	15 Shakespeare Way Casper, WY	82602
59.	2500 W. Chaucer St. Raleigh, NC	27601
60.	11R West Renoir Terrace Seattle, WA	98121-2526

List to Be Checked

Address	ZIP Code
2765 Avenelle Ave. Corning, NY	14830
2131B Windinall Lane Canton, OH	44720-7999
56 Brando Terrace Carlisle, PA	17013
15 Shakespeare Way Casper, WY	60282
2500 N. Chaucer St. Raleigh, NC	27601
11R West Renoir Terrace Seattle, WA	98121-2226

PART B: FORMS COMPLETION

30 Questions
15 Minutes

Directions: Read each form and answer the questions based on the information provided.

Questions 1–5 are based on the following information.

INSURED MAIL RECEIPT	
OFFICIAL USE	
1. Postage 　$	**2a.** ☐ Fragile　　**2b.** ☐ Perishable **2c.** ☐ Liquid　　**2d.** ☐ Hazardous
3. Insurance Fee	**4.** Insurance Coverage:
5. Special Handling Fee	**7.** Postmark Here
6. Total Postage & Fees 　$	
8. *Sent to:*	
9. *Street, Apt. No.; or PO Box No.*	
10. *City, State, ZIP + 4*®	

1.　Where would you enter the recipient's name?

    (A)　Box 2

    (B)　Box 3

    (C)　Box 8

    (D)　Box 10

2.　Which of these would be a correct entry for Box 2b?

    (A)　Post Office Box 202

    (B)　January 1, 2008

    (C)　Jean White

    (D)　A checkmark

3. Which would be a correct entry for Box 1?

   (A) 4:30 P.M.

   (B) $2.25

   (C) 03115

   (D) 10/4/08

4. In which box would the postmark be placed?

   (A) Box 2

   (B) Box 3

   (C) Box 7

   (D) Box 8

5. Where would you indicate the total postage cost?

   (A) Box 1

   (B) Box 5

   (C) Box 6

   (D) Box 8

Questions 6–10 are based on the following information.

DELIVERY CONFIRMATION RECEIPT
Postage and Delivery Confirmation fees must be paid before mailing
Article Sent To: (to be completed by mailer) *(Please Print Clearly)* **1.** Name
2. Street
3. City, State, ZIP+4

4. Postmark Here	POSTAL CUSTOMER: Keep this receipt.
	CHECK ONE (POSTAL USE ONLY) **5a.** ☐ Priority Mail™ Service **5b.** ☐ First-Class Mail® parcel **5c.** ☐ Package Services parcel

6. *DELIVERY CONFIRMATION NUMBER:*
0307   3330   0000   3758   9157

6. Where would you indicate Priority Mail service?

   (A) Box 5a

   (B) Box 5b

   (C) Box 5c

   (D) Box 6

7. Which would be a correct entry for Box 3?

   (A) John Marshall

   (B) 3456 Main St., Apt. 3D

   (C) (800) 555-1212

   (D) Pittsburgh, PA 15223

8. The delivery confirmation number can be found in which box?

    (A) Box 2

    (B) Box 3

    (C) Box 4

    (D) Box 6

9. Which would be a correct entry for Box 4?

    (A) Post office postmark

    (B) 232 Broadway

    (C) June 3, 2008

    (D) New York, NY 11021

10. According to the form, which is true?

    (A) For inquiries, the customer should access the U.S. Postal Service website.

    (B) Postage and delivery confirmation fees can be paid before mailing the parcel.

    (C) The customer does not need to keep the receipt.

    (D) The postal carrier should complete the mailer.

Questions 11–15 are based on the following information.

OFFICIAL MAIL FORWARDING CHANGE OF ADDRESS ORDER		
Please PRINT items 1-10 in blue or black ink. Your signature is required in item 9.		
1. Change of Address for: (Read Attached Instructions) □ Individual (#5) □ Entire Family (#5) □ Business (#6)	**2.** Is This Move Temporary? □ Yes □ No	
3. Start Date: (ex. 02/27/08)	**4.** If TEMPORARY move, print date to discontinue forwarding: (ex. 03/27/08)	
5a. LAST Name & Jr./Sr./etc.		
5b. FIRST Name and MI		
6. If BUSINESS Move, Print Business Name		
PRINT OLD MAILING ADDRESS BELOW: HOUSE/BUILDING NUMBER AND STREET NAME (INCLUDE ST., AVE., CT., ETC.) OR PO BOX		
7a. OLD Mailing Address		
7a. OLD APT or Suite	**7b.** For Puerto Rico Only: If address is in PR, print urbanization name, if appropriate.	
7c. OLD CITY	**7d.** State	**7e.** ZIP
PRINT NEW MAILING ADDRESS BELOW: HOUSE/BUILDING NUMBER, AND STREET NAME (INCLUDE ST., AVE., CT., ETC.) OR PO BOX		
8a. NEW Mailing Address		
8a. NEW APT/Ste or PMB	**8b.** For Puerto Rico Only: If address is in PR, print urbanization name, if appropriate.	
8c. NEW CITY	**8d.** State	**8e.** ZIP
9. Print and Sign Name (see conditions on reverse) Print: _____ Sign: _____	**10.** Date Signed: (ex. 01/27/08)	

11. Which of these would be a correct entry for Box 2?
    (A) 11/2/08
    (B) A checkmark
    (C) 29 Center St.
    (D) Chicago, IL 60602

12. Which is a correct entry for Box 6?
    (A) Educational Service Agency
    (B) Mr. Edward Jones
    (C) 09214-3333
    (D) Yes

13. In which box is a checkmark a correct entry?
    (A) Box 1
    (B) Box 4
    (C) Box 8a
    (D) Box 9

14. Which of these would be a correct entry for Box 7d?
    (A) 8/5
    (B) AZ
    (C) Phoenix
    (D) 08536

15. If the move is permanent, which box does NOT need to be completed?
    (A) Box 1
    (B) Box 2
    (C) Box 3
    (D) Box 4

Questions 16–21 are based on the following information.

EXPRESS MAIL

Post Office to Addressee

ORIGIN (POSTAL SERVICE USE ONLY)		
1. PO ZIP Code	**2.** Day of Delivery ☐ Next ☐ 2nd ☐ 2nd Del. Day	**3.** Postage $
4. Date Accepted Mo. Day Year	**5.** Scheduled Date of Delivery Month Day	**6.** Return Receipt Fee $
7. Time Accepted ☐ AM ☐ PM	**8.** Scheduled Time of Delivery ☐ Noon ☐ 3 PM	**9.** COD Fee $ **10.** Insurance Fee $
11. Military ☐ 2nd Day ☐ 3rd Day	**12.** Total Postage & Fees $	**13.** Flat Rate ☐ or Weight lbs. ozs.
14. Int'l Alpha Country Code	**15.** Acceptance Emp. Initials	

27. FROM: (PLEASE PRINT)   PHONE (   ) _____

DELIVERY (POSTAL USE ONLY)			
16. Delivery Attempt Mo. Day	**17.** Time	☐ AM ☐ PM	**18.** Employee Signature
19. Delivery Attempt Mo. Day	**20.** Time	☐ AM ☐ PM	**21.** Employee Signature
22. Delivery Date Mo. Day	**23.** Time	☐ AM ☐ PM	**24.** Employee Signature

CUSTOMER USE ONLY

25. PAYMENT BY ACCOUNT   Federal Agency Acct. No.
Express Mail Corporate   or Postal Service Acct. No.
Acct. No.

26. ☐ **WAIVER OF SIGNATURE** *(Domestic Mail Only)*
Additional merchandise insurance is void if customer requests waiver of signature.
I wish delivery to be made without obtaining signature of addressee or addressee's agent (if delivery employee judges that article can be left in secure location) and I authorize that delivery employee's signature constitutes valid proof of delivery.

NO DELIVERY   _____
☐ Weekend   Mailer Signature
☐ Holiday

28. TO: (PLEASE PRINT)   PHONE (   ) _____

ZIP + 4 (U.S. ADDRESSES ONLY. DO NOT USE FOR FOREIGN POSTAL CODES.)

☐ ☐ ☐ ☐ ☐ + ☐ ☐ ☐ ☐

FOR INTERNATIONAL DESTINATIONS, WRITE COUNTRY NAME BELOW.
29.

16. Which of these would be a correct entry for Box 13?

    (A) MWB

    (B) 13 lbs.

    (C) $16.50

    (D) 11:30

17. Which of these would be a correct entry for Box 15?

    (A) 215-665467

    (B) 08345

    (C) JMcC

    (D) 08536-1919

18. Where would the customer sign a signature waiver?

    (A) Box 18

    (B) Box 19

    (C) Box 20

    (D) Box 26

19. In which boxes would you indicate that the post office first attempted to deliver the package?

    (A) Boxes 16–18

    (B) Boxes 22–24

    (C) Boxes 25–26

    (D) Boxes 27–28

20. A customer is mailing a sample of his new product to Brazil. Where would he/she indicate the country name?

    (A) Box 25

    (B) Box 26

    (C) Box 28

    (D) Box 29

21. In which box would the customer enter the address of the person who will receive the package?

    (A) Box 24

    (B) Box 26

    (C) Box 27

    (D) Box 28

Questions 22–30 are based on the following information.

APPLICATION CARDS — PART 1

1. Name(s) to Which Box Number(s) is (are) Assigned	2. Box or Caller Numbers _____ through _____
3. Name of Person Applying. Title *(if representing an organization)*, and Name of Organization *(if Different From Item 1)*	4a. Will This Box Be Used for: ☐ Personal Use ☐ Business Use *(Optional)*
5. Address (Number, street, apt. no., city, state, and ZIP Code™). When address changes, cross out address here and put new address on back.	4b. Email Address *(Optional)*
	6. Telephone Number *(Include area code)*

7. Date Application Received	8. Box Size Needed	9. ID and Physical Address Verified by (Initials)	10. Dates of Service _____ through _____
11. Two types of identification are required. One must contain a photograph of the addressee(s). Social Security cards, credit cards, and birth certificates are unacceptable as identification. Write in identifying information. Subject to verification.		12. Check Eligibility for Carrier Delivery ☐ a. City ☐ b. Rural ☐ c. HCR ☐ d. None	13. Service assigned ☐ a. Box ☐ b. Caller ☐ c. Reserve No.
		14. List name(s) of minors or names of other persons receiving mail in individual box. Other persons must present two forms of valid ID. If applicant is a firm, name each member receiving mail. Each member must have verifiable ID upon request. *(Continue on reverse side.)*	

15. Signature of Applicant *(Same as Item 3)*. I agree to comply with all Postal Service® rules regarding Post Office box or caller services

APPLICATION CARDS — PART 2

Special Orders
16. Postmaster: The following named persons or representatives of the organization listed below are authorized to accept mail addressed to this (these) Post Office box(es) or caller number(s). All names listed must have verifiable ID. *(Continue on reverse side.)*

16a. Name of Box Customer *(Same as Item 1)*	16b. Name(s) of Applicant(s) *(Same as Item 3)*
16c. Other Authorized Representative	16d. Other Authorized Representative
17. Box or Caller Number to Which This Card Applies	20. Post Office Date Stamp
18. Will this box be used for Express Mail® reshipment? *(Check one)* a. Yes ☐ b. No ☐	

19. Signature of Applicant *(Same as Item 3)*. I agree to comply with all Postal Service® rules regarding Post Office box or caller services.

22. Which of these boxes should the customer complete?
    (A) Boxes 1–19
    (B) Boxes 1, 3–6, 14–16, and 18–19 only
    (C) Boxes 4–8 only
    (D) Boxes 9–19 only

23. Where would the customer enter his/her e-mail address?
    (A) Box 2
    (B) Box 4a
    (C) Box 4b
    (D) Box 9

24. In which box would 22.5″ × 12″ be a correct entry?
    (A) Box 2
    (B) Box 3
    (C) Box 8
    (D) Box 9

25. The customer's signature would be a correct entry in which box?
    (A) Box 5
    (B) Box 11
    (C) Box 14
    (D) Box 15

26. The name of the box customer should be entered in which of the following boxes?
    (A) Boxes 1 and 16a
    (B) Boxes 3 and 14
    (C) Boxes 15 and 16c
    (D) Boxes 14 and 19

27. Which of these would be a correct entry for Box 6?
    (A) dwhite@address.com
    (B) (732) 555-1212
    (C) P.O. Box 25
    (D) Trenton, NJ

28. Which of these would be a correct entry for Box 18?

    (A) The customer's signature

    (B) A checkmark

    (C) The post office date stamp

    (D) The box number

29. Which of these is NOT an acceptable form of identification for this application?

    (A) Passport

    (B) Driver's license

    (C) Corporate ID card

    (D) Social Security card

30. Which of these would be a correct entry for Box 14?

    (A) June 30–April 3

    (B) Post office date stamp

    (C) Sally Ross, Linda Seghers, Mandie Rosenberg, Heather McCarron

    (D) A checkmark

PART C: CODING AND MEMORY

Section 1: Coding

36 Questions
6 Minutes

Directions: Assign a code to questions 1–36 based on the coding guide below.

CODING GUIDE	
Address Range	**Delivery Route**
1–499 E. Sixth Ave. 500–599 N. Grand St. 11–199 N. Crystal Ln.	A
500–1500 E. Sixth Ave. 200–600 N. Crystal Ln.	B
600–800 N. Grand St. 20–100 King St. 1500–4500 S. Walker Rd.	C
All mail that doesn't fall in one of the address ranges listed above	D

	Address	Delivery Route			
1.	125 E. Sixth Ave.	A	B	C	D
2.	20 E. Sixth Ave.	A	B	C	D
3.	2503 S. Walker Rd.	A	B	C	D
4.	452 N. Crystal Ln.	A	B	C	D
5.	554 N. Grand St.	A	B	C	D
6.	31 King St.	A	B	C	D

	Address	Delivery Route			
7.	1465 S. Walker Rd.	A	B	C	D
8.	87 E. Sixth Ave.	A	B	C	D
9.	10 King St.	A	B	C	D
10.	708 N. Grand St.	A	B	C	D
11.	305 S. Crystal Ln.	A	B	C	D
12.	30 King St.	A	B	C	D
13.	399 N. Crystal Ln.	A	B	C	D
14.	300 E. Sixth Ave.	A	B	C	D
15.	2500 S. Walker Rd.	A	B	C	D
16.	25 Kang St.	A	B	C	D
17.	115 W. State St.	A	B	C	D
18.	799 N. Grand St.	A	B	C	D
19.	605 N. Crystal Ln.	A	B	C	D
20.	452 N. Grand St.	A	B	C	D
21.	450 E. Sixth Ave.	A	B	C	D
22.	4420 S. Walker Rd.	A	B	C	D
23.	710 N. Grand St.	A	B	C	D
24.	155 N. Crystal Ln.	A	B	C	D
25.	397 E. Sixth Ave.	A	B	C	D
26.	1500 N. Sixth Ave.	A	B	C	D
27.	52 King Ave.	A	B	C	D
28.	799 N. Grand St.	A	B	C	D
29.	4500 N. Walker Rd.	A	B	C	D
30.	564 N. Crystal Ln.	A	B	C	D
31.	24 King St.	A	B	C	D
32.	700 N. Grand St.	A	B	C	D
33.	77 S. King St.	A	B	C	D
34.	15-45 S. Walker Rd.	A	B	C	D
35.	542 N. Grand St.	A	B	C	D
36.	350 N. Crystal Ln.	A	B	C	D

Section 2: Memory

36 Questions
7 Minutes

Directions: Take three minutes to memorize the coding guide below. Assign a code based on your memory of the coding guide. This coding guide is the same guide used in the previous coding section.

CODING GUIDE	
Address Range	**Delivery Route**
1–499 E. Sixth Ave. 500–599 N. Grand St. 11–199 N. Crystal Ln.	A
500–1500 E. Sixth Ave. 200–600 N. Crystal Ln.	B
600–800 N. Grand St. 20–100 King St. 1500–4500 S. Walker Rd.	C
All mail that doesn't fall in one of the address ranges listed above	D

	Address	Delivery Route			
1.	3 E. Sixth Ave.	A	B	C	D
2.	299 N. Crystal Ln.	A	B	C	D
3.	600 N. Grand St.	A	B	C	D
4.	205 King St.	A	B	C	D
5.	110 E. Sixth Ave.	A	B	C	D
6.	400 N. Crystal Ln.	A	B	C	D
7.	4700 S. Walter Rd.	A	B	C	D

	Address	Delivery Route			
8.	200 N. Grand St.	A	B	C	D
9.	599 N. Grand St.	A	B	C	D
10.	310 N. Crystal Ln.	A	B	C	D
11.	6 Elsie St.	A	B	C	D
12.	50 King St.	A	B	C	D
13.	710 N. Grand St.	A	B	C	D
14.	500 N. Crystal Ln.	A	B	C	D
15.	650 N. Crystal Ln.	A	B	C	D
16.	50 N. Grand St.	A	B	C	D
17.	100 E. Sixth Ave.	A	B	C	D
18.	30 King St.	A	B	C	D
19.	345 N. Crystal St.	A	B	C	D
20.	1501 S. Walker Rd.	A	B	C	D
21.	199 N. Crystal Ln.	A	B	C	D
22.	90 King St.	A	B	C	D
23.	200 King St.	A	B	C	D
24.	400 N. Crystal Ln.	A	B	C	D
25.	2 N. Crystal Ln.	A	B	C	D
26.	920 E. Sixtieth St.	A	B	C	D
27.	5 E. Sixth Ave.	A	B	C	D
28.	1500 N. Ethel Ln.	A	B	C	D
29.	300 N. Crystal Ln.	A	B	C	D
30.	500 E. Sixth St.	A	B	C	D
31.	4023 S. Walker Rd.	A	B	C	D
32.	76 King St.	A	B	C	D
33.	199 E. Sixth Ave.	A	B	C	D
34.	245 N. Crystal Ln.	A	B	C	D
35.	1000 King St.	A	B	C	D
36.	3910 E. Sixth Ave.	A	B	C	D

Practice Test 3– 473/473c

ANSWER KEY

Part A: Address Checking

1.	C	21.	B	41.	C
2.	A	22.	B	42.	D
3.	B	23.	C	43.	D
4.	C	24.	B	44.	D
5.	B	25.	B	45.	A
6.	B	26.	A	46.	C
7.	B	27.	B	47.	B
8.	A	28.	C	48.	A
9.	B	29.	A	49.	B
10.	A	30.	B	50.	D
11.	B	31.	C	51.	D
12.	A	32.	A	52.	B
13.	D	33.	D	53.	C
14.	B	34.	B	54.	B
15.	B	35.	A	55.	A
16.	A	36.	B	56.	D
17.	A	37.	C	57.	B
18.	D	38.	D	58.	C
19.	B	39.	A	59.	B
20.	A	40.	A	60.	C

Part B: Forms Completion

1.	C	11.	B	21.	D
2.	D	12.	A	22.	B
3.	B	13.	A	23.	C
4.	C	14.	B	24.	C
5.	C	15.	D	25.	D
6.	A	16.	B	26.	A
7.	D	17.	C	27.	B
8.	D	18.	D	28.	B
9.	A	19.	A	29.	D
10.	A	20.	D	30.	C

Part C: Coding and Memory

Section 1: Coding

1.	A	13.	B	25.	A
2.	A	14.	A	26.	D
3.	C	15.	C	27.	C
4.	B	16.	D	28.	C
5.	A	17.	D	29.	D
6.	C	18.	C	30.	B
7.	D	19.	D	31.	C
8.	A	20.	D	32.	C
9.	D	21.	A	33.	D
10.	C	22.	C	34.	D
11.	D	23.	C	35.	A
12.	C	24.	A	36.	B

Section 2: Memory

1.	A	13.	C	25.	D
2.	B	14.	B	26.	D
3.	C	15.	D	27.	A
4.	D	16.	D	28.	D
5.	A	17.	A	29.	B
6.	B	18.	C	30.	B
7.	D	19.	B	31.	C
8.	D	20.	C	32.	C
9.	A	21.	A	33.	A
10.	B	22.	C	34.	B
11.	D	23.	D	35.	D
12.	C	24.	B	36.	D

POSTAL EXAMINATION 473/473c

PRACTICE TEST 4

Practice Test 4 – 473/473c

■ PART A: ADDRESS CHECKING

60 Questions
11 Minutes

Directions: Compare the **List to Be Checked** with the **Correct List**. Indicate if (A) there are **No Errors**, (B) there is an error in the **Address Only**, (C) there is an error in the **ZIP Code Only**, or (D) there is an error in **Both** the address and the ZIP code.

A. No Errors	B. Address Only	C. ZIP Code Only	D. Both

	Correct List			List to Be Checked	
	Address	*ZIP Code*		*Address*	*ZIP Code*
1.	5001 US Hwy. No. 46 Baltimore, MD	21202		5001 US Hwy. No. 46 Baltimore, MD	21202
2.	1 So. Martin Ave. Portland, OR	97214		1 So. Martin Ave. Portland, ME	97214
3.	4401 Clinton Ave. San Francisco, CA	94107		4041 Clinton Ave. San Francisco, CA	94701
4.	11 Progress Court Dayton, OH	45401		11 Progress St. Dayton, OH	45401
5.	US Hwy. 1 & Old Post Rd. Buffalo, NY	14216		US Hwy. 1 & Old Post Rd. Buffalo, NY	14612
6.	64 Plum St. Chicago, IL	60622		64 Plume St. Chicago, IL	60662

A. No Errors	B. Address Only	C. ZIP Code Only	D. Both

	Correct List			List to Be Checked	
	Address	*ZIP Code*		*Address*	*ZIP Code*
7.	861 South Ave. Washington, DC	20004		861 South Ave. Washington, DC	20004
8.	30J Montgomery Ct. Pismo Beach, CA	93448		305 Montgomery Ct. Pismo Beach, CA	93448
9.	62 Vernon Way Seattle, WA	98102		62 Vernon Way Seattle, WA	89102
10.	19 Princes Drive New York, NY	10014		19 Princess Drive New York, NY	14001
11.	14 Walker Ave. Chapel Hill, NC	27599		14 Walker Ave. Chapel Hill, NC	27599
12.	66L Claridge Place Steamboat Springs, CO	80477		661 Claridge Place Steamboat Springs, CO	80474
13.	14 Wysteria Dr. Indianapolis, IN	46253-1919		14 Wisteria Dr. Indianapolis, IN	46253-1919
14.	16 Dancaster Ct. Evergreen, CO	80437		6 Dancaster Ct. Evergreen, CO	80437
15.	926 Ellis Pkwy. Nashville, TN	37203		926 Ellis Pkwy. Nashville, TN	37203
16.	21B Oliver Ave. Baltimore, MD	21202		213 Oliver Ave. Baltimore, MD	21202
17.	224 Raymond Rd. Princeton, NJ	08540		224 Raymond Rd. Princeton, NJ	08540
18.	294 Bromley Place Buffalo, NY	11421		294 Browley Place Buffalo, NY	11421

| A. No Errors | B. Address Only | C. ZIP Code Only | D. Both |

Correct List   **List to Be Checked**

#	Address	ZIP Code	Address	ZIP Code
19.	100 McCaw Dr. Trenton, NJ	08618	100 McCaw Dr. Trenton, NJ	08638
20.	11 Phillips Dr. New York, NY	10027	111 Phillips Dr. New York, NY	12027
21.	47 Providence Blvd. San Francisco, CA	94107	47 Providence Rd. San Francisco, CA	94107
22.	166 Stafford Rd. Danville, VA	24511	16B Stafford Rd. Danville, VA	24115
23.	1 Gates Ave. West Miami, FL	33127	1 Gates Ave. West Miami, FL	31327
24.	28 June St. Memphis, TN	38117	28 July St. Memphis, TN	38117
25.	76 Kingsland Circle Tampa, FL	33601	76 Kingsland Circle Tampa, FL	33601
26.	46 Lewis Place Wilmington, DE	19850	46 Louis Place Wilmington, DE	19850
27.	140D Harding Ave. Brooklyn, NY	11213	140 Harding Ave. Brooklyn, NY	12113
28.	1 Chalet Drive Bridgeport, CT	06607	1 Chalet Drive Bridgeport, CT	00607
29.	8A Glynn Court Durham, NC	27707	8A Glynn Court Durham, NC	27707
30.	47 John F. Kennedy Dr. Annapolis, MD	21403	74 John F. Kennedy Dr. Annapolis, MD	21403

| A. No Errors | B. Address Only | C. ZIP Code Only | D. Both |

Correct List

	Address	ZIP Code
31.	37 Susan Lane Los Angeles, CA	90043
32.	213 S. Fulton St. El Paso, TX	79924
33.	201 West Locust Ave. Cheyenne, WY	82007
34.	128 Kane Ave. Lithonia, GA	30038
35.	24 Ernston Rd. Apt. 4 Philadelphia, PA	19131
36.	2104 N. Oaks Blvd. Montgomery, AL	36106
37.	16 Brown Ct. Landis, NC	28088
38.	11B Bayshore Dr. Frederick, MD	21701
39.	6 Cornwall Ct. Milwaukee, WI	53202
40.	37 Flagger Terrace Houston, TX	77006
41.	22 County Hwy. N. 516 Charleston, SC	29403
42.	3 Dennett Rd. Oklahoma City, OK	73102

List to Be Checked

Address	ZIP Code
37 Susan Place Los Angeles, CA	90043
213 S. Fulton St. El Paso, TX	79424
201 West Locust Ave. W. Cheyenne, WY	82007
128 Cane Ave. Lithonia, GA	30038
24 Earnest Rd. Apt. 4 Philadelphia, PA	19391
2104 N. Oaks Blvd. Montgomery, AL	36106
16 Brown Ct. Landis, NC	20888
11B Bayshore Dr. Fredericksburg, MD	21701
6 Cornwall St. Milwaukee, WI	53202
37 Flagger Terrace Houston, TX	77006
22 County Hwy. N. 561 Charlotte, NC	29403
3 Dennett Rd. Oklahoma City, OK	71302

A. No Errors	B. Address Only	C. ZIP Code Only	D. Both

	Correct List		List to Be Checked	

	Correct List		**List to Be Checked**	
	Address	ZIP Code	Address	ZIP Code
43.	20A Westminster Blvd. Tacoma, WA	98402	204 Westminster Blvd. Tacoma, WA	94082
44.	228 Dunhams Corner Rd. Staten Island, NY	10303	228 Dunhams Corner Rd. Staten Island, NY	10303
45.	10 W. Reed St. Norristown, PA	19404	10 W. Reed St. Norristown, PA	19404
46.	2 Angelika Ct. Sandpoint, ID	83864	2 Angelica Rd. Sandpoint, ID	83864
47.	24A Rossmoor Dr. Amherst, MA	01003-3910	24A Rossmoor Dr. Amherst, MA	01003-3910
48.	16 Tiger Lily Ct. Hillside, NJ	07205	16 Tiger Lily Ct. Hillside, NJ	07250
49.	2 Dogwood Dr. Greenville, MS	38701	2 Dogwood Dr. Greenville, MS	37801
50.	1463 Paunee Rd. Flagstaff, AZ	86001	1463 Pownee Rd. Flagstaff, AZ	80601
51.	151 Mary Ave. Flushing, NY	11367	151 Mary Ave. Flushing, WY	11367
52.	1388 Hollywood Ave. Alexandria, LA	71309	138B Hollywood Ave. Alexandria, LA	71309
53.	75 So. Rolph Place St. Louis, MO	63113	75 So. Rolph Place St. Louis, MO	63113
54.	40 Meadow Ct. Easton, PA	18042-1768	40 Meadow Ct. Easton, PA	18042-1768

| A. No Errors | B. Address Only | C. ZIP Code Only | D. Both |

Correct List

	Address	ZIP Code
55.	990C Aurora Rd. Glassboro, NJ	08028
56.	563 Park Dr. Iowa City, IA	52242
57.	2 N. Baldwin St. Arcata, CA	95521
58.	303 S. 2nd Ave. Berwyn, IL	60402
59.	10E East Garden Way New Haven, CT	06521
60.	12 N. 5th Ave. Apt. 2D Breckenridge, CO	80424

List to Be Checked

Address	ZIP Code
990C Aurena Rd. Glassboro, NJ	08028
563 Park Place Iowa City, IA	52242
2 N. Baldwin St. Arcata, CA	95251
303 S. 2nd Ave. Berwyn, IL	60402
10D East Garden Way New Haven, CT	06521
12 N. 5th Ave. Apt 2G Breckenridge, CO	80424

PART B: FORMS COMPLETION

30 Questions
15 Minutes

Directions: Read each form and answer the questions based on the information provided.

Questions 1–6 are based on the following information.

COD	
SAVE THIS RECEIPT	**See reverse side for claims information.**
1. Check Amount $	**2.** Cash Amount $
3a. ☐ Registered Mail **3b.** ☐ Express Mail® Service	**3c.** ☐ Form 3849-D Requested **3d.** _____ Date of Mailing
4. From:	**6.** To:
Check and Enter Amount *(If Applicable)* **5a.** ☐ Delivery Confirmation™ Service **5b.** ☐ Signature Confirmation™ Service	**5c.** ☐ Restricted Delivery **5e.** ☐ Return Receipt **5d.** ☐ Special Handling **5f.** Amt: _____
7. COD Fee	**8.** Postage	**9.** Postmark

1. Where would you indicate that the customer paid with cash?
    (A) Box 2
    (B) Box 3d
    (C) Box 4
    (D) Box 6

2. Which of these would be a correct entry for Box 3d?
    (A) Rural Route 3
    (B) A checkmark
    (C) Rusty Walker, 2 Main St., Anytown, PA
    (D) 7/22/08

3. Which would be a correct entry for Box 1?

    (A) 3:00 P.M.

    (B) $5.25

    (C) 08618

    (D) 9/2/08

4. In which box would the postal clerk enter the COD fee?

    (A) Box 1

    (B) Box 2

    (C) Box 7

    (D) Box 8

5. Where would you indicate that the customer wants a delivery confirmation?

    (A) Box 3a

    (B) Box 3c

    (C) Box 5a

    (D) Box 5d

6. A checkmark would be the correct entry for all of the following EXCEPT

    (A) Box 5a.

    (B) Box 5b.

    (C) Box 5e.

    (D) Box 5f.

Questions 7–11 are based on the following information.

STAMPS BY MAIL® ORDER FORM				
Please fill out clearly and completely.				

1. ☐☐☐ ☐☐☐☐☐☐☐
AREA CODE   DAYTIME PHONE NUMBER

2. _____
First Name   Middle Initial   Last Name

3. _____
Compay Name (if applicable)

4. _____
Mailing Address/PO Box   Apt./Suite

5. _____
City   State   ZIP+4®

ITEM	DESCRIPTION	PRICE	QTY.	COST
1	**Flag 24/7** 42¢ First-Class Roll(s) - 100 Stamps per roll	$42.00	**6.**	**7.**
2	**Forever Stamp** 42¢ First-Class Booklet(s) - 20 Stamps per booklet	$8.40	**8.**	**9.**
3	**Tiffany Lamp*** 1¢ Stamps - 20 Stamps	$.20	**10.**	**11.**
4	**Big Horn Sheep**** 17¢ Stamps - 10 Stamps	$1.70	**12.**	**13.**

*May be combined for the 42¢ First-Class price

**Additional ounce for First-Class price for Letter and Flat Mail

14. Total Cost of Order $ _____

7. Which of these would be a correct entry for Line 2?
   (A) Donna A. Phelps
   (B) Hammond Phelps Centre for Dance
   (C) Trenton, NJ 08618
   (D) (800) 123-4567

8. Where should the customer indicate that he/she wants to buy 20 Tiffany Lamp stamps?
   (A) Box 6
   (B) Box 8
   (C) Box 9
   (D) Box 10

9. Where would the customer indicate that the total paid was $42.00?
   (A) Box 6
   (B) Box 8
   (C) Box 12
   (D) Box 14

10. Which would be a correct entry for Box 5?
    (A) Ellington Hammond
    (B) 116 Village Boulevard
    (C) New York, NY 11021-1313
    (D) 555-1212

11. A dollar amount would be a correct entry for each box EXCEPT
    (A) Box 2.
    (B) Box 7.
    (C) Box 9.
    (D) Box 11.

Questions 12–16 are based on the following information.

CUSTOMS DECLARATION AND DISPATCH NOTE						
From Sender's Name Business Street City State ZIP+4® Country			Sender's Customs Reference *(if any)*	Insured Amount		
				Insured Fees (U.S. $)		SDR Value
To Addressee's Name Business Street Postcode City State/Province Country			Importer's Reference - Optional *(if any)* *(Tax code/VAT no./Importer code)*			
			Importer's Telephone/Fax/E-mail *(if known)*			
1. Detailed Description of Contents	**2.** Qty.	**3.** Net Weight lbs. oz.	**5.** Value (U.S. $)	*For Commerciial Senders Only*		
				7. HS Tarrif Number		**8.** Country of Origin of Goods
10. Check One ☐ Airmail/Priority ☐ Surface/Nonpriority	**4.** Total Gross Wt.		**6.** Total Value U.S. $	**9.** Total Postage and Fees		
11. Check One ☐ Gift ☐ Commercial Sample ☐ Merchandise Explanation: ☐ Documents ☐ Returned Goods ☐ Other				**17.** Sender's Instructions in Case of Nondelivery ☐ Treat as Abandoned ☐ Return to Sender NOTE: Item is subject to return charges at sender's expense. ☐ Redirect to Address Below:		Mailing Office Date Stamp
12. Comments *(e.g., goods subject to quarantine, sanitary/phytosanitary inspection, or other restrictions)*						
13. License Number(s)	**14.** Certificate Number(s)		**15.** Invoice Number			
16. Date and Sender's Signature						

12. Which of these would be a correct entry for Box 8?

    (A) A checkmark

    (B) Ghana

    (C) 3 pounds

    (D) Goods subject to quarantine

13. Where would you describe the contents of the package?

    (A) Box 1

    (B) Box 5

    (C) Box 11

    (D) Box 14

14. Where would you indicate that the package should be returned to the sender?

    (A) Box 11

    (B) Box 12

    (C) Box 16

    (D) Box 17

15. Which of these would be a correct entry for Box 16?

    (A) September 3, 2008

    (B) 9/3/08 and the sender's signature

    (C) 9/3 and the postmark

    (D) The sender's signature only

16. Which of these would be a correct entry for Box 11?

    (A) $23.00

    (B) (800) 555-1212

    (C) A checkmark

    (D) 4

Questions 17–21 are based on the following information.

RETURN RECEIPT FOR INTERNATIONAL MAIL		
Completed by the office of origin.	Item Description **1a.** ☐ Registered Article **1b.** ☐ Letter **1c.** ☐ Printed Matter **1d.** ☐ Other **1e.** ☐ Recorded Delivery **1f.** ☐ Express Mail International		
	2. ☐ Insured Parcel	**3.** Insured Value	**4.** Article Number
	5. Office of Mailing		**6.** Date of Posting
	7 Addressee Name or Firm		
	8. Street and No.		
	9. Place and Country		
Completed at destination.	This receipt must be signed by, (1) the addressee; or, (2) a person authorized to sign under the regulations of the country of destination; or, (3) if those regulations so provide, by the employee of the office of destination. This signed form will be returned to the sender by the first mail.		
	10. ☐ The article mentioned above was duly delivered.	**11.** Date	**14.** Postmark of the office of destination
	12. Signature of Addressee	**13.** Office of Destination Employee Signature	

17. Where would you indicate that Jim Brown wants to insure this package?

   (A) Box 1

   (B) Box 2

   (C) Box 4

   (D) Box 6

18. Where would you put a checkmark to indicate that the package contains printed matter?

   (A) Box 1a

   (B) Box 1b

   (C) Box 1c

   (D) Box 1f

19. Where would you indicate that the article was delivered?

    (A) Box 6
    (B) Box 10
    (C) Box 13
    (D) Box 14

20. You could enter a date in which of the following boxes?

    (A) Boxes 1 and 2
    (B) Boxes 3 and 5
    (C) Boxes 8 and 9
    (D) Boxes 6 and 11

21. Each of the following boxes should be completed at the office from which the article is sent EXCEPT

    (A) Box 1.
    (B) Box 6.
    (C) Box 7.
    (D) Box 14.

Questions 22–30 are based on the following information.

EMPLOYEE-GENERATED CHANGE OF ADDRESS
Please PRINT items 1-7 in blue or black ink. Your initials must be entered in box 6.
Change of Address for: **1a.** ☐ Individual   **1b.** ☐ Entire Family   **1c.** ☐ Business
2. Start Date: M M D D Y Y *(ex. 11/14/08)*

3a. Enter LAST or Business Name	**3b.** Enter FIRST Name & Middle Initial

PRINT **OLD** mailing address below *(Number and Street Name - Include ST, AVE, CT, etc. or PO Box number)*
4a. OLD Mailing Address

4b. OLD Apt. or Suite No.	**4c.** For Puerto Rico Only: Print urbanization name, if appropriate.

4d. OLD City Name	**4e.** State	**4f.** ZIP

5. ☐ MLNA (Moved, Left No Address)	☐ Box Closed (No Order)

6. Employee Initials	**7.** Date	**8.** Route ID Number

22. Which of these would be a correct entry for Box 1?

    (A) A checkmark

    (B) 35 Elsie Court, Chicago, IL 60612

    (C) 7:00 P.M.

    (D) $3.56

23. The customer has moved from 3 Main St, Canton, OH, to 432 Biscayne Blvd., Miami, FL. Where would you enter Canton?

    (A) Box 3b

    (B) Box 4d

    (C) Box 4e

    (D) Box 5

24. Where would you enter your initials?

    (A) Box 3a

    (B) Box 5

    (C) Box 6

    (D) Box 8

25. You could enter a checkmark in each of the following boxes EXCEPT

    (A) Box 1a.

    (B) Box 1b.

    (C) Box 5.

    (D) Box 8.

26. Which of these would be a correct entry for Box 4f?

    (A) 08536-1919

    (B) 08536

    (C) 11/14/03

    (D) NJ

27. How would you indicate that the change of address is for a family?

    (A) Put a checkmark in Box 1b.

    (B) Put a checkmark in Box 1c.

    (C) Complete Box 3a.

    (D) Complete Box 3b.

28. Where would you indicate that the business has not left a forwarding address?

    (A) Box 5

    (B) Box 6

    (C) Box 7

    (D) Box 8

29. Which of these would be a correct entry for Box 2?

    (A) January 11, 2009

    (B) 01/11/09

    (C) 1/11/2009

    (D) Jan. 11, 2009

30. Where would you indicate that the postal route ID number is 435A?

    (A) Box 3b

    (B) Box 4c

    (C) Box 6

    (D) Box 8

 PART C: CODING AND MEMORY

Section 1: Coding

36 Questions
6 Minutes

Directions: Assign a code to questions 1–36 based on the coding guide below.

CODING GUIDE	
Address Range	**Delivery Route**
2100–3599 Hyde St. 1200–2899 Shirley Rd. 100–899 N. Dover Ave.	A
4100–5699 Hyde St. 2900–3500 Shirley Rd.	B
600–800 New Market St. 4100–5699 W. Riva Ct. 900–1699 N. Dover Ave.	C
All mail that doesn't fall in one of the address ranges listed above	D

Address	Delivery Route			
1. 3200 Hyde St.	A	B	C	D
2. 4200 W. Riva Ct.	A	B	C	D
3. 5400 Hyde St.	A	B	C	D
4. 4299 S. Riva Ct.	A	B	C	D
5. 344 N. Dover Ave.	A	B	C	D
6. 767 New Market St.	A	B	C	D
7. 3984 Shirley Rd.	A	B	C	D
8. 546 N. Dover Ave.	A	B	C	D
9. 1699 S. Dover Ave.	A	B	C	D
10. 743 New Market St.	A	B	C	D
11. 3154 Shirley Rd.	A	B	C	D
12. 5344 Hyde St.	A	B	C	D
13. 455 N. Dover Ave.	A	B	C	D
14. 2644 Shirley Rd., Apt 9E	A	B	C	D
15. 300 Dover St.	A	B	C	D
16. 678 New Market St.	A	B	C	D
17. 4677 W. Riva Ct.	A	B	C	D
18. 3598 Hyde St.	A	B	C	D
19. 5555 Hyde St.	A	B	C	D
20. 678 New Market St.	A	B	C	D
21. 455 N. Dover Ave.	A	B	C	D
22. 599 New Market Ct.	A	B	C	D
23. 5322 W. Riva Ct.	A	B	C	D
24. 3211 Shirley Rd.	A	B	C	D
25. 3266 Hyde St.	A	B	C	D
26. 1244 N. Dover Ave.	A	B	C	D
27. 5699 W. River Ct.	A	B	C	D
28. 3501 Shirley Rd.	A	B	C	D
29. 4823 Hyde St.	A	B	C	D
30. 1678 Shirley Rd.	A	B	C	D
31. 645 New Market St.	A	B	C	D

	Address	Delivery Route			
32.	3165 Shirley Rd.	A	B	C	D
33.	1467 N. Dover Ave.	A	B	C	D
34.	169 N. Dover Ave.	A	B	C	D
35.	2987-B Hyde St.	A	B	C	D
36.	3422 Shirley Rd.	A	B	C	D

Section 2: Memory

36 Questions
7 Minutes

Directions: Take three minutes to memorize the coding guide below. Assign a code based on your memory of the coding guide. This coding guide is the same guide used in the previous coding section.

CODING GUIDE	
Address Range	**Delivery Route**
2100–3599 Hyde St. 1200–2899 Shirley Rd. 100–899 N. Dover Ave.	A
4100–5699 Hyde St. 2900–3500 Shirley Rd.	B
600–800 New Market St. 4100–5699 W. Riva Ct. 900–1699 N. Dover Ave.	C
All mail that doesn't fall in one of the address ranges listed above	D

Address	Delivery Route			
1. 800 River Rd.	A	B	C	D
2. 299 N. Dover Ave.	A	B	C	D
3. 600 New Market St.	A	B	C	D
4. 2900 Shirley Rd.	A	B	C	D
5. 1200 Shirley Rd.	A	B	C	D
6. 4101 W. Riva Ct.	A	B	C	D
7. 4700 Hyde St.	A	B	C	D
8. 200 New Market St.	A	B	C	D
9. 399 N. Dover Ave.	A	B	C	D
10. 4699 W. Riva Ct.	A	B	C	D
11. 3095 Shirley Rd.	A	B	C	D
12. 900 Dover Ave.	A	B	C	D
13. 710 N. Dover Ave.	A	B	C	D
14. 500 New Market St.	A	B	C	D
15. 3133 Shirley Rd.	A	B	C	D
16. 5000 Hyde St.	A	B	C	D
17. 1249 Shirley Rd.	A	B	C	D
18. 3000 Hyde St.	A	B	C	D
19. 4500 Old Market St.	A	B	C	D
20. 4322 W. Riva Ct.	A	B	C	D
21. 789 New Market St.	A	B	C	D
22. 4200 Hyde St.	A	B	C	D
23. 453 N. Dover Ave.	A	B	C	D
24. 5689 W. Riva Ct.	A	B	C	D
25. 655 New Market St.	A	B	C	D
26. 1200 Cheryl Rd.	A	B	C	D
27. 5600 Hyde St.	A	B	C	D
28. 2977 Shirley Rd.	A	B	C	D
29. 1699 Dover Ave. S	A	B	C	D
30. 754 New Market St.	A	B	C	D
31. 600 Mark Ave.	A	B	C	D

	Address	Delivery Route			
32.	754-32 N. Dover Ave.	A	B	C	D
33.	2600 Hyde St.	A	B	C	D
34.	4987 W. Riva Ct.	A	B	C	D
35.	2922 Shirley Rd.	A	B	C	D
36.	3910 N. Dover Ave.	A	B	C	D

Practice Test 4 – 473/473c

Part A: Address Checking

1.	A	21.	B	41.	B
2.	B	22.	D	42.	C
3.	D	23.	C	43.	D
4.	B	24.	B	44.	A
5.	C	25.	A	45.	A
6.	D	26.	B	46.	B
7.	A	27.	D	47.	A
8.	B	28.	C	48.	C
9.	C	29.	A	49.	C
10.	D	30.	B	50.	D
11.	A	31.	B	51.	B
12.	D	32.	C	52.	B
13.	B	33.	B	53.	A
14.	B	34.	B	54.	A
15.	A	35.	D	55.	B
16.	B	36.	A	56.	B
17.	A	37.	C	57.	C
18.	B	38.	B	58.	A
19.	C	39.	B	59.	B
20.	D	40.	A	60.	B

Part B: Forms Completion

1. A
2. D
3. B
4. C
5. C
6. D
7. A
8. D
9. D
10. C

11. A
12. B
13. A
14. D
15. B
16. C
17. A
18. C
19. B
20. D

21. D
22. A
23. B
24. C
25. D
26. B
27. A
28. A
29. B
30. D

Part C: Coding and Memory

Section 1: Coding

1. A
2. C
3. B
4. D
5. A
6. C
7. B
8. A
9. D
10. C
11. B
12. B

13. A
14. A
15. D
16. C
17. C
18. A
19. B
20. C
21. A
22. D
23. C
24. B

25. A
26. C
27. D
28. D
29. B
30. A
31. C
32. B
33. C
34. A
35. A
36. B

Section 2: Memory

1.	D	13.	A	25.	C
2.	A	14.	D	26.	D
3.	C	15.	B	27.	B
4.	B	16.	B	28.	B
5.	A	17.	A	29.	D
6.	C	18.	A	30.	C
7.	B	19.	D	31.	D
8.	D	20.	C	32.	A
9.	A	21.	C	33.	A
10.	C	22.	B	34.	C
11.	B	23.	A	35.	B
12.	D	24.	C	36.	D

POSTAL EXAMINATION 473/473c

PRACTICE TEST 5

Practice Test 5– 473/473c

PART A: ADDRESS CHECKING

60 Questions
11 Minutes

Directions: Compare the **List to Be Checked** with the **Correct List**. Indicate if (A) there are **No Errors**, (B) there is an error in the **Address Only**, (C) there is an error in the **ZIP Code Only**, or (D) there is an error in **Both** the address and the ZIP code.

A. No Errors	B. Address Only	C. ZIP Code Only	D. Both

Correct List

	Address	ZIP Code
1.	125 North St. Branchport, NY	14418
2.	53 Chantilly Lane Dover, NH	03821
3.	1915 First Ave. Auburn, AL	36832
4.	275 River Road Juneau, AK	99803
5.	9 Saddle Brook Ct. Roxbury, VT	05669
6.	7652 Bakers Lane Alexander, IA	50420

List to Be Checked

	Address	ZIP Code
1.	125 North Ave. Branchport, NY	14118
2.	53 Chantilly Lane Dover, NH	03281
3.	1915 First Ave. Auburn, MA	36833
4.	275 River Road Juneau, AK	99803
5.	9 Saddle Brook Ct. Roxbury, VT	05669
6.	7652 Bakers Lane Alexandria, IA	50420

A. No Errors	B. Address Only	C. ZIP Code Only	D. Both

Correct List

	Address	ZIP Code
7.	568 Southwest Place Clarion, PA	16214
8.	13000 Main Blvd. Secretary, MD	21664
9.	17 NW 8th St. Danielson, CT	06239
10.	546 Eastwick Pkwy. Warren, ME	04864
11.	37 Spring Valley Court Marysville, OH	43040
12.	670 Newton Lane Louisburg, NC	27549
13.	10122 Gast 40th St. Clewiston, FL	33440
14.	31-15 Willow Ave. Reedville, VA	22539
15.	21-07 Sussex Rd. Hagarstown, IL	62247
16.	407 Country Blvd. Smoaks, SC	29481
17.	23 Quentin Way Crawford, WV	26343
18.	257 Washington St. Portsmouth, RI	02871

List to Be Checked

Address	ZIP Code
568 Southwest Place Clarion, PA	16214
13000 Main Blvd. Secretary, MD	26164
17 SW 8th St. Danielson, CT	06236
546 Eastwick Pkwy. Warren, ME	04684
37 Spring Alley Court Marysville, OH	43040
670 Newton Lane Lewisburg, NC	24975
10122 East 40th St. Clewiston, FL	33440
31-51 Willow Ave. Reedville, VA	22539
21-07 Sussex Rd. Hagerstown, IN	62247
407 Country Blvd. Smoaks, SC	29481
23 Quentin Way Crawfield, WV	26443
275 Washington St. Portsmouth, RI	02871

A. No Errors	B. Address Only	C. ZIP Code Only	D. Both

	Correct List			**List to Be Checked**	
	Address	*ZIP Code*		*Address*	*ZIP Code*
19.	56-03 Ethel Road West Piscataway, NJ	08854		56-03 Ethel Road West Piscataway, NJ	08954
20.	1996 Fullerton Ave. Oakdale, TN	37829		1996 Fullerton Ave. Oakdale, TN	37829
21.	826 Sleepy Hollow Way Blue Bell, PA	19422		826 Sleepy Gallows Way Blue Bell, PA	19242
22.	127 Parkway West Sunflower, MS	38778		127 Parkway West Sunflower, MI	37878
23.	58A South Broad St. Thomaston, GA	30286		58A South Broad St. Thomaston, GA	30286
24.	3-18 Parrot Blvd. Jonesville, KY	41052		3-18 Parrot Blvd. Jamesville, KY	41052
25.	72M North Avenue Baton Rouge, LA	70826		72N North Avenue Baton Rouge, LA	70628
26.	7 Centennial Parkway Pine Bluff, AR	71601		7 Centennial Parkway Pine Bluff, AR	71609
27.	45 Apple Tree Drive Cheyenne, WY	82009		45 Apple Tree Drive Cheyenne, WY	82090
28.	10-05 Avon Street Carleton, NE	68326		10-05 Avon Street Carletown, NE	68326
29.	1215 Gardenview Place Ponderosa, NM	87044		1215 Gardenfield Place Ponderosa, NM	87044
30.	5H Linus Drive Chippewa Lake, MI	49320		5H Linus Drive Chippewa Lake, MI	42390

| A. No Errors | B. Address Only | C. ZIP Code Only | D. Both |

Correct List

	Address	ZIP Code
31.	2690 Mary Lynn Rd. Lyndon Station, WI	53944
32.	87 Horse Neck Way St. Louis, MO	63017
33.	431-B Wishing Well Ave. San Antonio, TX	78211
34.	9 Hardscrabble Place Norman, OK	73026
35.	19 Casserole Street Pearl Harbor, HI	96860
36.	141-02 Basket Court Roslyn, NY	11576
37.	71-D Youngs Parkway Brattleboro, VT	05301
38.	25 Camelback Avenue Valdosta, GA	31605
39.	678 Julius Caesar Rd. Selbyville, DE	19975
40.	10K Royal Run Ct. Two Rivers, AK	99716
41.	3-81 Woodland St. Hightstown, NJ	08520
42.	189 Eighth Ave. Harrisburg, PA	17108-1995

List to Be Checked

Address	ZIP Code
2690 Mary Lynn Dr. Lyndon Station, WI	53944
87 Horse Neck Way St. Louis, MO	63017
431-B Wishing Will Ave. San Antonio, TX	78211
9 Hardscrapple Place Norman, OK	75026
19 Casserole Street Pearl Harbor, HI	98680
141-02 Basket Court Rozlyn, NY	11576
71-D Youngs Parkway Brattleboro, VT	05301
25 Camelotback Avenue Valdosta, GA	31605
678 Julius Caesar Rd. Shelbyville, DE	19775
10K Royal Run Ct. Two Rivers, AK	99716
3-18 Woodland St. Hightstown, NJ	08520
189 Eighth Ave. Harrisburg, PA	17108-1959

A. No Errors	B. Address Only	C. ZIP Code Only	D. Both

<table>
<tr><td colspan="3">**Correct List**</td><td colspan="2">**List to Be Checked**</td></tr>
<tr><td></td><td>*Address*</td><td>*ZIP Code*</td><td>*Address*</td><td>*ZIP Code*</td></tr>
<tr><td>43.</td><td>72 Brussel Sprout Blvd. Wilmington, DE</td><td>19886-5715</td><td>72 Brussel Stout Blvd. Wilmington, DE</td><td>19886-5715</td></tr>
<tr><td>44.</td><td>2119 Manning Way Pfeifer, KS</td><td>67660</td><td>2119 Manning Way Pfeifer, KS</td><td>67660</td></tr>
<tr><td>45.</td><td>44 Melrose Street Glastonbury, CT</td><td>06033</td><td>44 Melrose Street Glastorbury, CT</td><td>06030</td></tr>
<tr><td>46.</td><td>951 Zydecko Line Rd. Highgate Falls, VT</td><td>05459</td><td>951 Zydecko Line Rd. Highgate Falls, VT</td><td>04559</td></tr>
<tr><td>47.</td><td>16-2 Wyomissing Ave. Kahului, HI</td><td>96733</td><td>16-2 Wyoming Ave. Kahului, HI</td><td>96373</td></tr>
<tr><td>48.</td><td>462 NW 11th St. Washington, DC</td><td>20538</td><td>462 NW 12th St. Washington, DC</td><td>20538</td></tr>
<tr><td>49.</td><td>7523 Stanton Hwy. Bloomfield, CT</td><td>06002</td><td>7532 Stanton Hwy. Bloomfield, CT</td><td>06002</td></tr>
<tr><td>50.</td><td>4 Timber Tree Court Missoula, MT</td><td>59804</td><td>4 Timber Tree Court Missoula, MT</td><td>59814</td></tr>
<tr><td>51.</td><td>92 East Main Street Cranford, NJ</td><td>07016</td><td>92 East Main Street Cranford, NH</td><td>07016</td></tr>
<tr><td>52.</td><td>185 Mills Creek Highway Baltimore, MD</td><td>21297-1464</td><td>185 Hills Creek Highway Baltimore, MD</td><td>21797-1464</td></tr>
<tr><td>53.</td><td>91 Twisted Iron Place Mount Vernon, SD</td><td>57363</td><td>91 Twisted Iron Street Mount Vernon, SD</td><td>57366</td></tr>
<tr><td>54.</td><td>6217 Eleventh St. Santa Fe Springs, CA</td><td>90670</td><td>6217 Eleventh St. Santa Fe Strings, CA</td><td>90670</td></tr>
</table>

A. No Errors	B. Address Only	C. ZIP Code Only	D. Both

	Correct List			List to Be Checked	

	Address	*ZIP Code*	*Address*	*ZIP Code*
55.	61 Roanoke Ave. Tacoma, WA	98455	61 Roanoke Ave. Tacoma, WA	98445
56.	5 Four Corners Blvd. Chattanooga, TN	37409-0219	5 Four Corners Blvd. Chattenooga, TN	37409-0219
57.	3212 Rising Sun Ct. Claymont, DE	19703	3212 Rising Sun Ct. Claymont, DE	17903
58.	29 Tennis Court Way Litchville, ND	58461	29 Tennis Court Way Litchville, ND	58461
59.	331 Central Mountain Ave. Reston, VA	20191-1502	331 Center Mountain Ave. Reston, VA	20119-1502
60.	71 Snowcap Place Greeley, CO	80634	71 Snowcap Place Greeley, CA	80634

PART B: FORMS COMPLETION

30 Questions
15 Minutes

Directions: Read each form and answer the questions based on the information provided.

Questions 1–8 are based on the following information.

PAYMENT FORM		
1. Last Name	**2.** First Name	**3.** Middle Initial
4. Street Address		
5. City	**6.** State	**7.** ZIP Code

8. Date_____
   8a. Month _____
   8b. Day _____
   8c. Year _____
		9. Amount Paid
		   $ _____

10. Payment Method (Check One)
   10a. Check ☐
   10b. Money Order ☐
   10c. Cash ☐
   10d. Credit Card ☐		

1. If a person's name is John K. Logan, where should the letter K be placed?

   (A) Box 1

   (B) Box 2

   (C) Box 3

   (D) Box 4

2. Susan Riggs wishes to make a payment of $100 by using a money order. In which box should she place a checkmark?

   (A) Box 10a

   (B) Box 10b

   (C) Box 10c

   (D) Box 10d

3. Which one of the following is a correct entry for Box 8c?

    (A) $150.10

    (B) June

    (C) 31

    (D) 2008

4. Which one of the following is NOT a correct entry for Box 6?

    (A) Maine

    (B) Idaho

    (C) Atlanta

    (D) Florida

5. Randy Jones lives on 6 Main St., Tempe, Arizona 85282. Which entry belongs in Box 7?

    (A) 85282

    (B) 6

    (C) Main St.

    (D) Tempe

6. Rebecca Kipling is making a payment of $50 on August 10, 2009. In which box should "August" be placed?

    (A) Box 2

    (B) Box 8a

    (C) Box 5

    (D) Box 8c

7. Marianne V. Welding lives in Bound Brook, New Jersey. In which box should "Marianne" be placed?

    (A) Box 5

    (B) Box 1

    (C) Box 3

    (D) Box 2

8. Which one of the following is a correct entry for Box 4?

    (A) Williams

    (B) 9 Crescent Way

    (C) Iowa

    (D) 08536

Questions 9–16 are based on the following information.

ATTEMPTED DELIVERY NOTICE	
1. Today's Date	**3a.** Sender's Name
2. Date Item(s) Sent	**3b.** Sender's Address
4. ☐ If checked, someone must be present to sign for item(s).	

5. Enter Number of Each
  5a. ____ Letter
  5b. ____ Magazine or Catalog
  5c. ____ Large Envelope
  5d. ____ Box
	6. Postage
	  6a. ☐ If checked, there is postage
	       due on item(s).
	  6b. ☐ _____ Amount due

7. Delivery
  7a. ☐ Item(s) will be redelivered tomorrow.
  7b. ☐ Please pick up the item(s) at your local Post Office.
       The item(s) will be available after
  7c. Date _____ **7d.** Time _____	

9. Which box would be checked if a magazine has postage due?

    (A) Box 4

    (B) Box 6a

    (C) Box 7a

    (D) Box 7b

10. If a delivery was attempted for two magazines, in which box would "2" appear?

    (A) Box 5c

    (B) Box 5a

    (C) Box 5d

    (D) Box 5b

11. Which of the following would be a correct entry for Box 3b?

    (A) 12 Main St., Boise, Idaho 83701

    (B) T. J. Smith

    (C) $1.20

    (D) Nov. 3, 2008

12. How would you indicate that three letters and two boxes are to be delivered?

    (A) Enter "3" in Box 5a and enter "2" in Box 5c.

    (B) Enter "3" in Box 5c and enter "2" in Box 5b.

    (C) Enter "3" in Box 5d and enter "2" in Box 5b.

    (D) Enter "3" in Box 5a and enter "2" in Box 5d.

13. In which boxes would a date appear?

    (A) Only in Boxes 1 and 2

    (B) Only in Boxes 1, 2, and 4

    (C) Only in Boxes 1, 2, and 7c

    (D) Only in Boxes 7b and 7c

14. Suppose a letter was not deliverable on June 1, and assume that June 1 is today's date. The addressee was then notified that he could pick up the letter at the local post office after June 2 at 1:00 P.M. Which of the following is completely correct?

    (A) Enter "June 1" in Box 1 and enter "June 2" in Box 2.

    (B) Enter "June 1" in Box 7c and enter "1:00 P.M." in Box 7d.

    (C) Enter "June 2" in Box 7c and enter "1:00 P.M." in Box 7d.

    (D) Enter "June 2" in Box 1 and enter "1:00 P.M." in Box 7c.

15. Which one of the following could appear in Box 6b?

    (A) May 1

    (B) $1.75

    (C) 4:00 P.M.

    (D) Mary Williams

16. If a large envelope is not deliverable on a specific day but will be redelivered the following day, which boxes should be filled in and/or checked?
    (A) Boxes 5c and 7a
    (B) Boxes 5c and 7b
    (C) Boxes 5a and 7a
    (D) Boxes 5a and 7b

Questions 17–24 are based on the following information.

MASS MAILING RECEIPT	
1. Date	**4.** Name of Permit Holder
2. Post Office ZIP Code	**5.** Address of Permit Holder
3. 5-digit Permit Number	**6.** Phone Number of Permit Holder
7. Processing Category (Check one) **7a.** ☐ Letters **7b.** ☐ Flats **7c.** ☐ Automation Flats **7d.** ☐ Parcels	**8.** Total Number of Pieces

	9. Total Weight
	  9a. _____ pounds
	  9b. _____ ounces

	10. 2-digit Cost Code
	11. Total Paid $ _____

17. If the permit holder's five-digit number is 01736, in which box should this number be entered?
    (A) Box 3
    (B) Box 6
    (C) Box 8
    (D) Box 10

18. An item that costs $4.20 has a cost code of 38. Which one of the following is completely correct?

   (A) Enter "$4.20" in Box 8 and enter "38" in Box 10.

   (B) Enter "$4.20" in Box 11 and enter "38" in Box 10.

   (C) Enter "$4.20" in Box 10 and enter "38" in Box 8.

   (D) Enter "$4.20" in Box 10 and enter "38" in Box 11.

19. If the total weight of a mailing is 8 pounds 4 ounces, in which box should you place a "4"?

   (A) Box 8

   (B) Box 9a

   (C) Box 9b

   (D) Box 11

20. Which one of the following is an appropriate entry for Box 2?

   (A) 08527

   (B) 31

   (C) 11/03/08

   (D) $1.50

21. If a mailing consists of six letters, seven flats, and twelve parcels, what number should be entered in Box 8?

   (A) 12

   (B) 19

   (C) 25

   (D) 30

22. If Jason Donnelly is the owner of a mass mailing permit, in which box would you find his name?

   (A) Box 6

   (B) Box 3

   (C) Box 5

   (D) Box 4

23. If Boxes 7b and 7d are checked, what is being mailed?

    (A) Flats and parcels

    (B) Flats and automation flats

    (C) Letters and flats

    (D) Automation flats and parcels

24. Which one of the following is an appropriate entry for Box 10?

    (A) 41275

    (B) 9063

    (C) 175

    (D) 81

Questions 25–30 are based on the following information.

RETURN RECEIPT REQUEST	
1. Article Addressed To	**2.** Signature
	3. Received By (Printed Name)
	4. Date of Delivery

5. Service Type
   5a. ☐ Certified Mail
   5b. ☐ Registered Mail
   5c. ☐ Insured Mail
	5d. ☐ Express Mail
	5e. ☐ Return Receipt for Merchandise
	5f. ☐ C.O.D.

6. Restricted Delivery?
   6a. ☐ Yes
   6b. ☐ No
	7. Is delivery address different from Box 1?
	   7a. ☐ Yes **7b.** ☐ No
	If Yes, enter delivery address below.

8. Article Number	

25. If an article is express mail, which box should be checked?
    (A) Box 5d
    (B) Box 5c
    (C) Box 5b
    (D) Box 5a

26. Which one of the following boxes requires a number?
    (A) Box 2
    (B) Box 5
    (C) Box 6
    (D) Box 8

27. Box 6b would be checked to indicate that
    (A) the article is registered.
    (B) the article is C.O.D.
    (C) there is no restricted delivery.
    (D) there is restricted delivery.

28. If an article is addressed to 12 Franklin Street but is delivered to 25 Franklin Street, which box must be checked?
    (A) Box 5c
    (B) Box 7a
    (C) Box 5d
    (D) Box 7b

29. If Nancy Porter receives this form, where should she sign her name?
    (A) Box 3
    (B) Box 8
    (C) Box 2
    (D) Box 7

30. Which one of the following would NOT appear in Box 4?
    (A) Month
    (B) Date
    (C) Year
    (D) Time

PART C: CODING AND MEMORY

Section 1: Coding

36 Questions
6 Minutes

Directions: Assign a code to questions 1–36 based on the coding guide below.

CODING GUIDE	
Address Range	**Delivery Route**
1–300 South Blvd. 10–49 Main Ave. 20–99 U.S. Route 2	A
50–150 Main Ave. 100–500 U.S. Route 2 5–30 Ryan Lane	B
80–800 33rd Street 1000–5000 Cheshire Way 31–80 Ryan Lane	C
All mail that doesn't fall in one of the address ranges listed above	D

	Address	Delivery Route			
1.	36 Ryan Lane	A	B	C	D
2.	4500 Cheshire Way	A	B	C	D
3.	225 Main Ave.	A	B	C	D
4.	130 US Route 2	A	B	C	D
5.	19 Ryan Lane	A	B	C	D

	Address	Delivery Route			
6.	900 Cheshire Way	A	B	C	D
7.	21 US Route 2	A	B	C	D
8.	48 Main Ave.	A	B	C	D
9.	55 Cheshire Way	A	B	C	D
10.	481 South Blvd.	A	B	C	D
11.	7 Ryan Lane	A	B	C	D
12.	3200 Cheshire Way	A	B	C	D
13.	91 US Route 2	A	B	C	D
14.	721 33rd Street	A	B	C	D
15.	47 Ryan Lane	A	B	C	D
16.	14 Main Ave.	A	B	C	D
17.	1000 33rd Street	A	B	C	D
18.	6000 Cheshire Way	A	B	C	D
19.	88 Ryan Lane	A	B	C	D
20.	61 Main Ave.	A	B	C	D
21.	2222 Cheshire Way	A	B	C	D
22.	420 US Route 2	A	B	C	D
23.	52 US Route 2	A	B	C	D
24.	101 Main Ave.	A	B	C	D
25.	601 33rd Street	A	B	C	D
26.	500 South Blvd.	A	B	C	D
27.	75 33rd Street	A	B	C	D
28.	35 Main Ave.	A	B	C	D
29.	23 US Route 2	A	B	C	D
30.	3045 Cheshire Way	A	B	C	D
31.	28 Ryan Lane	A	B	C	D
32.	582 US Route 2	A	B	C	D
33.	16 South Blvd.	A	B	C	D
34.	65 33rd Street	A	B	C	D
35.	15 Ryan Lane	A	B	C	D
36.	741 33rd Street	A	B	C	D

Section 2: Memory

36 Questions
7 Minutes

Directions: Take three minutes to memorize the coding guide below. Assign a code based on your memory of the coding guide. This coding guide is the same guide used in the previous coding section.

CODING GUIDE	
Address Range	**Delivery Route**
1–300 South Blvd. 10–49 Main Ave. 20–99 U.S. Route 2	A
50–150 Main Ave. 100–500 U.S. Route 2 5–30 Ryan Lane	B
80–800 33rd Street 1000–5000 Cheshire Way 31–80 Ryan Lane	C
All mail that doesn't fall in one of the address ranges listed above	D

	Address	Delivery Route			
1.	4120 Cheshire Way	A	B	C	D
2.	11 US Route 2	A	B	C	D
3.	3 Ryan Lane	A	B	C	D
4.	88 33rd Street	A	B	C	D
5.	260 South Blvd.	A	B	C	D
6.	62 33rd Street	A	B	C	D

	Address	Delivery Route			
7.	25 Ryan Lane	A	B	C	D
8.	1111 Cheshire Way	A	B	C	D
9.	32 Ryan Lane	A	B	C	D
10.	202 US Route 2	A	B	C	D
11.	180 South Blvd.	A	B	C	D
12.	6161 Cheshire Way	A	B	C	D
13.	800 33rd Street	A	B	C	D
14.	140 Main Ave.	A	B	C	D
15.	10 Main Ave.	A	B	C	D
16.	3500 Cheshire Way	A	B	C	D
17.	69 33rd Street	A	B	C	D
18.	68 Ryan Lane	A	B	C	D
19.	4 Main Ave.	A	B	C	D
20.	307 South Blvd.	A	B	C	D
21.	30 Ryan Lane	A	B	C	D
22.	4900 Cheshire Way	A	B	C	D
23.	75 Main Ave.	A	B	C	D
24.	807 33rd Street	A	B	C	D
25.	15 South Blvd.	A	B	C	D
26.	26 US Route 2	A	B	C	D
27.	31 Ryan Lane	A	B	C	D
28.	105 US Route 2	A	B	C	D
29.	999 Cheshire Way	A	B	C	D
30.	30 Main Ave.	A	B	C	D
31.	310 South Blvd.	A	B	C	D
32.	121 Main Ave.	A	B	C	D
33.	13 Ryan Lane	A	B	C	D
34.	2553 Cheshire Way	A	B	C	D
35.	40 Ryan Lane	A	B	C	D
36.	778 33rd Street	A	B	C	D

Practice Test 5 – 473/473c

ANSWER KEY

Part A: Address Checking

1.	D	21.	D	41.	B
2.	C	22.	D	42.	C
3.	D	23.	A	43.	B
4.	A	24.	B	44.	A
5.	A	25.	D	45.	D
6.	B	26.	C	46.	C
7.	A	27.	C	47.	D
8.	C	28.	B	48.	B
9.	D	29.	B	49.	B
10.	C	30.	C	50.	C
11.	B	31.	B	51.	B
12.	D	32.	A	52.	D
13.	B	33.	B	53.	D
14.	B	34.	D	54.	B
15.	B	35.	C	55.	C
16.	A	36.	B	56.	B
17.	D	37.	A	57.	C
18.	B	38.	B	58.	A
19.	C	39.	D	59.	D
20.	A	40.	A	60.	B

Part B: Forms Completion

1.	C	11.	A	21.	C
2.	B	12.	D	22.	D
3.	D	13.	C	23.	A
4.	C	14.	C	24.	D
5.	A	15.	B	25.	A
6.	B	16.	A	26.	D
7.	D	17.	A	27.	C
8.	B	18.	B	28.	B
9.	B	19.	C	29.	C
10.	D	20.	A	30.	D

Part C: Coding and Memory

Section 1: Coding

1.	C	13.	A	25.	C
2.	C	14.	C	26.	D
3.	D	15.	C	27.	D
4.	B	16.	A	28.	A
5.	B	17.	D	29.	A
6.	D	18.	D	30.	C
7.	A	19.	D	31.	B
8.	A	20.	B	32.	D
9.	D	21.	C	33.	A
10.	D	22.	B	34.	D
11.	B	23.	A	35.	B
12.	C	24.	B	36.	C

Section 2: Memory

1.	C	13.	C	25.	A
2.	D	14.	B	26.	A
3.	D	15.	A	27.	C
4.	C	16.	C	28.	B
5.	A	17.	D	29.	D
6.	D	18.	C	30.	A
7.	B	19.	D	31.	D
8.	C	20.	D	32.	B
9.	C	21.	B	33.	B
10.	B	22.	C	34.	C
11.	A	23.	B	35.	C
12.	D	24.	D	36.	C

POSTAL EXAMINATION 473/473c

PRACTICE TEST 6

Practice Test 6 – 473/473c

 PART A: ADDRESS CHECKING

60 Questions
11 Minutes

Directions: Compare the **List to Be Checked** with the **Correct List**. Indicate if (A) there are **No Errors**, (B) there is an error in the **Address Only**, (C) there is an error in the **ZIP Code Only**, or (D) there is an error in **Both** the address and the ZIP code.

A. No Errors	B. Address Only	C. ZIP Code Only	D. Both

Correct List

	Address	ZIP Code
1.	27 Towers Road Laupahoehoe, HI	96764
2.	14 Brook Lane Duck Creek Village, UT	84762
3.	712 Cristy Street Bryant Pond, ME	04219
4.	3 Finger Lake Drive Aberdeen, MD	21001
5.	4-A Market Avenue Grosse Pointe, MI	48230
6.	5-B Calculator Place Moorefield, ME	69039

List to Be Checked

Address	ZIP Code
27 Powers Road Laupahoehoe, HI	96746
14 Brook Lane Duck Creek Village, UT	84762
712 Crystal Street Bryant Pond, ME	04219
3 Finger Lake Drive Aberdene, MD	21010
4-A Market Avenue Grosse Pointe, MI	48230
5-B Calculator Road Moorefield, NE	60939

A. No Errors	B. Address Only	C. ZIP Code Only	D. Both

Correct List			**List to Be Checked**		
	Address	*ZIP Code*		*Address*	*ZIP Code*
7.	891 Valley Boulevard Lewiston, ID	83501		819 Valley Boulevard Lewiston, ID	83501
8.	34 Forest Avenue East Tylertown, MS	39667		34 Forest Avenue East Tylertown, MS	39677
9.	8 Spring Court Montrose, AR	71658		8 Spring Court Montrose, AR	71658
10.	6-C Hollow Point Way Graniteville, VT	05654		6-C Hollow Point Way Grantville, VT	05654
11.	78 Mattress Place Pomerene, AZ	85627		78 Mattress Place Pomerene, AZ	85626
12.	1962 Covenant Road Parmelee, SD	57566		1926 Covenant Road Parmelee, SD	57656
13.	12F Slope Junction Road Zanesville, OH	43701		12F Slope Junction Road Zanesville, OK	47301
14.	3287 Reading Avenue South Willow Springs, MO	65793		3287 Reading Avenue South Willow Strings, MO	65793
15.	28-D Rustlers Circle Mauldin, SC	29662		28-G Rustlers Circle Mauldin, SC	29662
16.	963 West 4th Street Van Dyne, WI	54979		963 West 4th Street Van Dyne, WI	54799
17.	56 Apt. 13 1st Avenue Kenderhook, IL	62345		56 Apt. 13 1st Avenue Kenderhook, IL	62345
18.	125 South 22nd Place Rosebud, MT	59347		125 North 22nd Place Rosebud, MT	54397

A. No Errors	B. Address Only	C. ZIP Code Only	D. Both

	Correct List			List to Be Checked	
	Address	ZIP Code		Address	ZIP Code
19.	656 Hunting Bow Lane Saint Georges, DE	19733		656 Hunters Bow Lane Saint Georges, DE	19733
20.	2147 Van Wyck Parkway Windsor Locks, CT	06096		2147 Van Wick Parkway Windsor Locks, CT	06996
21.	82-35 Second Road Imlaystown, NJ	08526		82-53 Second Road Imlaystown, NJ	08625
22.	14 Avalanche Way Horsepen, VA	24619		14 Avalanche Way Horsepet, VA	24619
23.	9-P Creek Alley Street Alderson, OK	74522		9-P Creek Alley Street Alderson, OK	74252
24.	7 Spinning Wheel Drive Osnabrock, ND	58269		7 Spinning Well Drive Osnabrock, ND	58269
25.	1-18 Fox Valley Court Peachtree City, GA	30269		1-18 Fox Valley Court Peachtree City, CA	30269
26.	59 Pedigree Street Jennerstown, PA	15547		59 Pedigree Street Jennerstown, PA	15547
27.	654 Manalapan Way Manitoa Springs, CO	80829		654 Manalapan Way Manitoa Springs, CO	80289
28.	7921 Raritan Bay Drive Teton Village, WY	83025		7921 Raritan Bay Drive Seton Village, WY	83015
29.	92 Sidewalk Circle Tellico Plains, TN	37385		92 Sidewall Circle Tellico Plains, TN	37385
30.	815 West 45th Avenue Deer River, NY	13627		815 West 46th Avenue Deer River, NY	16327

A. No Errors	B. Address Only	C. ZIP Code Only	D. Both

	Correct List		List to Be Checked	
	Address	ZIP Code	Address	ZIP Code
31.	6254 Turtle Boulevard Austin, TX	78758-7929	6524 Turtle Boulevard Austin, TX	78758-7929
32.	19-C McAllister Street Center Sandwich, NH	03227	19-E McAllister Street Center Sandwich, NH	02327
33.	290 Rocky Hill Highway Drewsey, OR	97904	290 Rocky Hill Highway Drewsey, OR	97904
34.	9 Shark Landing Place Medical Lake, WA	99022	9 Shark Landing Place Medicine Lake, WA	99022
35.	15 Eighth Avenue North Narragansett, RI	02882	15 Eighteenth Avenue North Narragansett, RI	02882
36.	57 McDuffy Lane Tallahassee, FL	32303-6106	57 MacDuffy Lane Tallahassee, FL	32303-6016
37.	191 Vanderbilt Road Willard, NM	87063	191 Vanderbilt Road Willard, NM	87064
38.	2 Spruce Tree Court Biloxi, MS	39534-2494	2 Spruce Tree Court Biloxi, MS	34594-2494
39.	51 Ace Club Street Gardnerville, NV	89410	51 Ace Club Street Gardenville, NV	89410
40.	8 N.E. Central Road Fairmont, NC	28340	8 N.E. Central Road Fairmont, NC	28340
41.	632 Sugar Shack Avenue Nerstrand, MN	55053	632 Sugar Shank Avenue Nerstrand, MN	55503
42.	15 Song Way East Walpole, MA	02032	15 Song Way East Walpole, MA	02023

A. No Errors	B. Address Only	C. ZIP Code Only	D. Both

	Correct List			List to Be Checked	

	Address	ZIP Code		Address	ZIP Code
43.	62 Evening Court North Wilmington, DE	19807-3021		62 Evening Count North Wilmington, DE	19807-3021
44.	17 N.W. Fifth Road Big Spring, TX	79720		17 N.W. Fifth Road Big Spring, TX	77920
45.	23-D Zee Street Old Fields, WV	26845		23-D Zee Street Old Fields, WV	26845
46.	10 Rising Moon Circle West Memphis, AR	72301-4302		10 Rising Moon Circle West Memphis, AL	72301-4302
47.	93 S.E. 6th Road Hollidaysburg, PA	16648		93 S.E. 6th Road Hollidaysburg, PA	16684
48.	57 Renegade Lane Cottonport, LA	71327		57 Renegades Lane Cottonport, LA	71327
49.	456-H Frozen Boulevard Pontiac, MI	48340-2805		465-H Frozen Boulevard Pontiac, MI	48340-2803
50.	12 High Top Avenue Lake Isabella, CA	93240		12 High Top Avenue Lake Isabella, CA	93240
51.	39 Football Highway Hawkeye, IA	52147		39 Football Highway Hawkeye, IA	52147
52.	48-2 Enterprise Way Grenola, KS	67346		48-2 Enterprise Way Grenola, KS	67436
53.	16-J Winterspoon Street Jasonville, IN	47438		16-J Winterspool Street Jasonville, IN	47738
54.	26 Mason Drive Columbia, SC	29201-4256		26 Mason Drive Columbia, SC	29201-4526

A. No Errors	B. Address Only	C. ZIP Code Only	D. Both

Correct List

	Address	ZIP Code
55.	123 Crescent Lane Sleetmute, AK	99668
56.	21-51 Gravel Road Horseshoe Bend, ID	83629
57.	872 Idle Engine Court Flatwoods, KY	41139
58.	3 Picadilly Lane Ocean View, DE	19970
59.	38-B 54th Road West Walnut Grove, MS	39189
60.	20 Sand Rock Street Laughlin, NV	89029

List to Be Checked

Address	ZIP Code
123 Cresent Lane Sleetmute, AK	99668
21-15 Gravel Road Horseshoe Bend, ID	82639
872 Island Engine Court Flatwoods, KY	43119
3 Picadilly Lane Oceans View, DE	19970
38-B 45th Road West Walnut Grove, MS	38189
20 Sand Rock Street Laughlin, NV	89029

PART B: FORMS COMPLETION

30 Questions
15 Minutes

Directions: Read each form and answer the questions based on the information provided.

Questions 1–10 are based on the following information.

PAYMENT FORM		
1. Last Name	**2.** First Name	**3.** Middle Initial
4. Street Address		
5. City	**6.** State	**7.** ZIP Code
8. Phone Number	**9.** E-mail Address	

10. Today's Date
    10a. Month _____
    10b. Day _____
    10c. Year _____

11. Amount Paid
    $ _____

12. Payment Method (Check one)
    12a. Check ☐
    12b. Money order ☐
    12c. Cash ☐
    12d. Credit card ☐

13. If Box 12d is checked, write the credit card number

_____

1. Linda R. Scott would write her last name in which box?

    (A) Box 1

    (B) Box 2

    (C) Box 3

    (D) Box 4

2. Melinda Williams is making a payment of $40 in cash. Which one of the following is correct?

    (A) "$40" is entered in Box 11, and Box 12a is checked.

    (B) "Melinda" is entered in Box 2, and Box 12c is checked.

    (C) "Williams" is entered in Box 3, and Box 12c is checked.

    (D) "$40" is entered in Box 8, and Box 12a is checked.

3. Bob Jackson is making a $100 payment on September 10, 2008. In which box would the number "10" appear?

   (A) Box 10c

   (B) Box 10a

   (C) Box 11

   (D) Box 10b

4. Roger Lewis lives on 15 Valley Road in Guttenberg, IA 52052. Which of the following belongs in Box 7?

   (A) 15

   (B) 52052

   (C) Roger

   (D) Lewis

5. Which one of the following is NOT a correct entry for Box 6?

   (A) Ohio

   (B) Georgia

   (C) Miami

   (D) New Jersey

6. Which box, if checked, requires a follow-up entry in Box 13?

   (A) Box 12b

   (B) Box 12a

   (C) Box 12d

   (D) Box 12c

7. Which of the following would be a correct entry for Box 9?

   (A) wsmith@yahoo.com

   (B) Indiana

   (C) January

   (D) 21 South Street

8. Which one of the following should NOT contain any digits?

   (A) Box 4

   (B) Box 8

   (C) Box 7

   (D) Box 5

9. If a person does not have a middle name, which box would necessarily be blank?

   (A) Box 2

   (B) Box 3

   (C) Box 6

   (D) Box 8

10. What is the MAXIMUM number of digits allowed in Box 10b?

    (A) 1

    (B) 2

    (C) 3

    (D) 4

Questions 11–18 are based on the following information.

ATTEMPTED DELIVERY NOTICE	
1. Today's Date	**2.** Date Item(s) Sent

3. Sender's Name	**4.** Sender's Address
	   4a. Street
	
	   4b. City
	
	   4c. State and ZIP Code

5. Enter Number of Each
   5a. ____ Letter(s)
   5b. ____ Magazine(s)
   5c. ____ Catalog(s)
   5d. ____ Other(s)	

6. Postage
   6a. ☐ If checked, there is postage due on item(s)
   6b. _____ Amount Due	

7. Delivery
   7a. ☐ Item(s) will be redelivered next weekday.
   7b. ☐ Please pick up the item(s) at your local post office.
       The item(s) will be available after:
   7c. Date: _____   Time: _____
   7d. ☐ If checked, someone must be present to sign for item(s).	

11. If Box 5d is filled in, which of the following items could have been sent?

    (A) A catalog

    (B) An envelope

    (C) A letter

    (D) A magazine

12. If an item is to be picked up at a local post office after June 4, 2008, at "1:00 P.M.," where would the entry of "1:00 P.M." be placed?

    (A) Box 1

    (B) Box 6b

    (C) Box 7c after "Date"

    (D) Box 7c after "Time"

13. Which of the following is a correct entry for Box 4C?

    (A) Michelle Brown

    (B) New Jersey 08512

    (C) 19 Market Avenue

    (D) August 5, 2008

14. What is a valid reason for a checkmark in Box 6a?

    (A) Sender's name is missing.

    (B) Postage is correct.

    (C) Postage is due.

    (D) Sender's address is missing.

15. Which box should be checked if someone must be present to sign for the item being delivered?

    (A) Box 7d

    (B) Box 7a

    (C) Box 6a

    (D) Box 5d

16. Which of the following would NOT contain a number?

    (A) Box 5b

    (B) Box 1

    (C) Box 2

    (D) Box 4b

17. Suppose that the date of the attempted delivery notice is Friday, July 20, 2007. If no one is present to sign for the item, which of the following (assuming redelivery) is correct?

    (A) Box 7d is checked, and the item will be redelivered on July 21.

    (B) Box 7d is checked, and the item will be redelivered on July 23.

    (C) Box 7a is checked, and the item will be redelivered on July 21.

    (D) Box 7a is checked, and the item will be redelivered on July 23.

18. Which of the following would be a correct entry for Box 6b?

    (A) April 5

    (B) 14539

    (C) $3.50

    (D) Chicago

Questions 19–25 are based on the following information.

MASS MAILING RECEIPT	
1. Today's Date **1a.** Month _____ **1b.** Day _____ **1c.** Year _____	**7.** Processing Category (Check all that apply) **7a.** ☐ Letters **7b.** ☐ Flats **7c.** ☐ Parcels **7d.** ☐ Boxes
2. Name of Permit Holder	
3. Street Address	**8.** Total Number of Pieces
4. City, State, ZIP Code	**9.** Total Weight _____ pounds, _____ ounces
5. Phone Number	**10.** Two-Digit Cost Code
6. Five-digit Permit Number	**11.** Total Paid

19. Which box would always contain five digits?

    (A) Box 6

    (B) Box 5

    (C) Box 10

    (D) Box 11

20. If a mailing consists of nine letters, four flats, and eight boxes, what number should be entered in Box 8?

    (A) 19

    (B) 20

    (C) 21

    (D) 22

21. Which of the following is an appropriate entry for Box 3?

    (A) 75214

    (B) John Adams

    (C) 3-B Central Avenue

    (D) 215-678-9110

22. Ten parcels and three letters, total weight 5 pounds, 6 ounces, are mailed. Which one of the following is correct?

    (A) Enter "13" in Box 8, and check one box in Box 7.

    (B) Enter "5" and "6" in Box 9, and check two boxes in Box 7.

    (C) Enter "13" in Box 9, and check two boxes in Box 7.

    (D) Enter "5" and "6" in Box 8, and check one box in Box 7.

23. Which one of the following would NOT appear in Box 1?

    (A) 30

    (B) 2005

    (C) July

    (D) Scranton

24. In which box would a number such as 35 NEVER appear?

    (A) Box 5

    (B) Box 8

    (C) Box 9

    (D) Box 10

25. Which one of the following is an appropriate entry for Box 2?

    (A) $8.60

    (B) Rhode Island

    (C) 18 Atlantic Street

    (D) Kathleen Brown

Questions 26–30 are based on the following information.

RETURN RECEIPT REQUEST	
1. Article Addressed To	**2.** Signature
	3. Received By (Print Name)
	4. Date of Delivery

5. Service Type
  5a. ☐ Certified Mail
  5b. ☐ Registered Mail
  5c. ☐ Insured Mail
	5d. ☐ Express Mail
	  5e. ☐ C.O.D.
	  5f. ☐ Returned Goods

6. Restricted Delivery?
  6a. ☐ Yes
  6b. ☐ No
	7. Is delivery address different
	  from Box 1?
	  7a. ☐ Yes **7b.** ☐ No

8. Article Number	**9.** If Box 7A is checked enter the delivery address

10. Postage Due?
  10a. ☐ No
  10b. ☐ Yes
  Amount _____	

26. If an article has restricted delivery and postage is due, which boxes must be checked?
    (A) Boxes 6a and 10a
    (B) Boxes 6a and 10b
    (C) Boxes 6b and 10a
    (D) Boxes 6b and 10b

27. An article is addressed to 5 Maple Lane, but it is delivered to 15 Maple Lane. Which box must be checked?
    (A) Box 7b
    (B) Box 7a
    (C) Box 6a
    (D) Box 6b

28. If Box 5c is checked, the article being delivered is
    (A) insured mail.
    (B) C.O.D.
    (C) Returned goods.
    (D) Certified Mail.

29. Which of the following could NOT appear in Box 4?
    (A) October
    (B) 2008
    (C) 8
    (D) William

30. If an article is Express Mail with restricted delivery, which boxes must be checked?
    (A) Boxes 5d and 6b
    (B) Boxes 5a and 6a
    (C) Boxes 5d and 6a
    (D) Boxes 5a and 6b

PART C: CODING AND MEMORY

Section 1: Coding

36 Questions
6 Minutes

Directions: Assign a code to questions 1–36 based on the coding guide below.

CODING GUIDE	
Address Range	**Delivery Route**
1–199 West Road 10–59 Demarest Ave. 30–99 Route 10	A
200–499 West Road 100–139 Route 10	B
60–129 Demarest Ave. 140–299 Route 10 11–89 Sunset Way	C
All mail that doesn't fall in one of the address ranges listed above	D

	Address	Delivery Route			
1.	211 West Road	A	B	C	D
2.	99 Sunset Way	A	B	C	D
3.	18 Demarest Ave.	A	B	C	D
4.	120 Route 10	A	B	C	D
5.	465 West Road	A	B	C	D
6.	152 Route 10	A	B	C	D

	Address	Delivery Route			
7.	145 Demarest Ave.	A	B	C	D
8.	37 Sunset Way	A	B	C	D
9.	61 Demarest Ave.	A	B	C	D
10.	193 West Road	A	B	C	D
11.	101 Route 10	A	B	C	D
12.	508 West Road	A	B	C	D
13.	57 Demarest Ave.	A	B	C	D
14.	24 Route 10	A	B	C	D
15.	93 Sunset Way	A	B	C	D
16.	304 West Road	A	B	C	D
17.	128 Route 10	A	B	C	D
18.	8 Demarest Ave.	A	B	C	D
19.	143 Route 10	A	B	C	D
20.	517 West Road	A	B	C	D
21.	10 Sunset Way	A	B	C	D
22.	136 Route 10	A	B	C	D
23.	16 West Road	A	B	C	D
24.	72 Route 10	A	B	C	D
25.	111 Route 10	A	B	C	D
26.	32 Sunset Way	A	B	C	D
27.	121 Demarest Ave.	A	B	C	D
28.	285 West Road	A	B	C	D
29.	44 Demarest Ave.	A	B	C	D
30.	13 Sunset Way	A	B	C	D
31.	400 Route 10	A	B	C	D
32.	7 Sunset Way	A	B	C	D
33.	250 West Road	A	B	C	D
34.	98 Route 10	A	B	C	D
35.	86 Demarest Ave.	A	B	C	D
36.	40 West Road	A	B	C	D

Section 2: Memory

36 Questions
7 Minutes

Directions: Take three minutes to memorize the coding guide below. Assign a code based on your memory of the coding guide. This coding guide is the same guide used in the previous coding section.

CODING GUIDE	
Address Range	**Delivery Route**
1–199 West Road 10–59 Demarest Ave. 30–99 Route 10	A
200–499 West Road 100–139 Route 10	B
60–129 Demarest Ave. 140–299 Route 10 11–89 Sunset Way	C
All mail that doesn't fall in one of the address ranges listed above	D

	Address		Delivery Route		
1.	131 Route 10	A	B	C	D
2.	393 West Road	A	B	C	D
3.	11 Sunset Way	A	B	C	D
4.	55 Route 10	A	B	C	D
5.	226 West Road	A	B	C	D
6.	171 West Road	A	B	C	D

	Address	Delivery Route			
7.	139 Route 10	A	B	C	D
8.	23 Demarest Ave.	A	B	C	D
9.	67 West Road	A	B	C	D
10.	82 Sunset Way	A	B	C	D
11.	3 Sunset Way	A	B	C	D
12.	112 Demarest Ave.	A	B	C	D
13.	84 Route 10	A	B	C	D
14.	6 Demarest Ave.	A	B	C	D
15.	68 Sunset Way	A	B	C	D
16.	123 Route 10	A	B	C	D
17.	95 Demarest Ave.	A	B	C	D
18.	16 Route 10	A	B	C	D
19.	36 Demarest Ave.	A	B	C	D
20.	425 West Road	A	B	C	D
21.	41 Route 10	A	B	C	D
22.	170 Sunset Way	A	B	C	D
23.	600 West Road	A	B	C	D
24.	53 Demarest Ave.	A	B	C	D
25.	119 West Road	A	B	C	D
26.	74 Sunset Way	A	B	C	D
27.	107 Route 10	A	B	C	D
28.	201 Route 10	A	B	C	D
29.	134 Demarest Ave.	A	B	C	D
30.	55 West Road	A	B	C	D
31.	90 Route 10	A	B	C	D
32.	108 Demarest Ave.	A	B	C	D
33.	104 Sunset Way	A	B	C	D
34.	345 West Road	A	B	C	D
35.	25 Demarest Ave.	A	B	C	D
36.	19 Route 10	A	B	C	D

Practice Test 6 – 473/473c

▋ANSWER KEY

Part A: Address Checking

1.	D	21.	D	41.	D
2.	A	22.	B	42.	C
3.	B	23.	C	43.	B
4.	D	24.	B	44.	C
5.	A	25.	B	45.	A
6.	D	26.	A	46.	B
7.	B	27.	C	47.	D
8.	C	28.	D	48.	B
9.	A	29.	B	49.	D
10.	B	30.	D	50.	A
11.	C	31.	B	51.	A
12.	D	32.	D	52.	C
13.	D	33.	A	53.	D
14.	B	34.	B	54.	C
15.	B	35.	B	55.	B
16.	C	36.	D	56.	D
17.	A	37.	C	57.	D
18.	D	38.	C	58.	B
19.	B	39.	B	59.	D
20.	D	40.	A	60.	A

Part B: Forms Completion

1. A	11. B	21. C
2. B	12. D	22. B
3. D	13. B	23. D
4. B	14. C	24. A
5. C	15. A	25. D
6. C	16. D	26. B
7. A	17. D	27. B
8. D	18. C	28. A
9. B	19. A	29. D
10. B	20. C	30. C

Part C: Coding and Memory

Section 1: Coding

1. B	13. A	25. B
2. D	14. D	26. C
3. A	15. D	27. C
4. B	16. B	28. B
5. B	17. B	29. A
6. C	18. D	30. C
7. D	19. C	31. D
8. C	20. D	32. D
9. C	21. D	33. B
10. A	22. B	34. A
11. B	23. A	35. C
12. D	24. A	36. A

Section 2: Memory

1.	B	13.	A	25.	A
2.	B	14.	D	26.	C
3.	C	15.	C	27.	B
4.	A	16.	B	28.	C
5.	B	17.	C	29.	D
6.	A	18.	D	30.	A
7.	B	19.	A	31.	A
8.	A	20.	B	32.	C
9.	A	21.	A	33.	D
10.	C	22.	D	34.	B
11.	D	23.	D	35.	A
12.	C	24.	A	36.	D

POSTAL EXAMINATION 473/473c

ANSWER SHEETS

POSTAL EXAM 473/473c
ANSWER SHEET

■ PRACTICE TEST 1: ADDRESS CHECKING

1. Ⓐ Ⓑ Ⓒ Ⓓ	21. Ⓐ Ⓑ Ⓒ Ⓓ	41. Ⓐ Ⓑ Ⓒ Ⓓ
2. Ⓐ Ⓑ Ⓒ Ⓓ	22. Ⓐ Ⓑ Ⓒ Ⓓ	42. Ⓐ Ⓑ Ⓒ Ⓓ
3. Ⓐ Ⓑ Ⓒ Ⓓ	23. Ⓐ Ⓑ Ⓒ Ⓓ	43. Ⓐ Ⓑ Ⓒ Ⓓ
4. Ⓐ Ⓑ Ⓒ Ⓓ	24. Ⓐ Ⓑ Ⓒ Ⓓ	44. Ⓐ Ⓑ Ⓒ Ⓓ
5. Ⓐ Ⓑ Ⓒ Ⓓ	25. Ⓐ Ⓑ Ⓒ Ⓓ	45. Ⓐ Ⓑ Ⓒ Ⓓ
6. Ⓐ Ⓑ Ⓒ Ⓓ	26. Ⓐ Ⓑ Ⓒ Ⓓ	46. Ⓐ Ⓑ Ⓒ Ⓓ
7. Ⓐ Ⓑ Ⓒ Ⓓ	27. Ⓐ Ⓑ Ⓒ Ⓓ	47. Ⓐ Ⓑ Ⓒ Ⓓ
8. Ⓐ Ⓑ Ⓒ Ⓓ	28. Ⓐ Ⓑ Ⓒ Ⓓ	48. Ⓐ Ⓑ Ⓒ Ⓓ
9. Ⓐ Ⓑ Ⓒ Ⓓ	29. Ⓐ Ⓑ Ⓒ Ⓓ	49. Ⓐ Ⓑ Ⓒ Ⓓ
10. Ⓐ Ⓑ Ⓒ Ⓓ	30. Ⓐ Ⓑ Ⓒ Ⓓ	50. Ⓐ Ⓑ Ⓒ Ⓓ
11. Ⓐ Ⓑ Ⓒ Ⓓ	31. Ⓐ Ⓑ Ⓒ Ⓓ	51. Ⓐ Ⓑ Ⓒ Ⓓ
12. Ⓐ Ⓑ Ⓒ Ⓓ	32. Ⓐ Ⓑ Ⓒ Ⓓ	52. Ⓐ Ⓑ Ⓒ Ⓓ
13. Ⓐ Ⓑ Ⓒ Ⓓ	33. Ⓐ Ⓑ Ⓒ Ⓓ	53. Ⓐ Ⓑ Ⓒ Ⓓ
14. Ⓐ Ⓑ Ⓒ Ⓓ	34. Ⓐ Ⓑ Ⓒ Ⓓ	54. Ⓐ Ⓑ Ⓒ Ⓓ
15. Ⓐ Ⓑ Ⓒ Ⓓ	35. Ⓐ Ⓑ Ⓒ Ⓓ	55. Ⓐ Ⓑ Ⓒ Ⓓ
16. Ⓐ Ⓑ Ⓒ Ⓓ	36. Ⓐ Ⓑ Ⓒ Ⓓ	56. Ⓐ Ⓑ Ⓒ Ⓓ
17. Ⓐ Ⓑ Ⓒ Ⓓ	37. Ⓐ Ⓑ Ⓒ Ⓓ	57. Ⓐ Ⓑ Ⓒ Ⓓ
18. Ⓐ Ⓑ Ⓒ Ⓓ	38. Ⓐ Ⓑ Ⓒ Ⓓ	58. Ⓐ Ⓑ Ⓒ Ⓓ
19. Ⓐ Ⓑ Ⓒ Ⓓ	39. Ⓐ Ⓑ Ⓒ Ⓓ	59. Ⓐ Ⓑ Ⓒ Ⓓ
20. Ⓐ Ⓑ Ⓒ Ⓓ	40. Ⓐ Ⓑ Ⓒ Ⓓ	60. Ⓐ Ⓑ Ⓒ Ⓓ

POSTAL EXAM 473/473c
ANSWER SHEET

PRACTICE TEST 1: FORMS COMPLETION

1. Ⓐ Ⓑ Ⓒ Ⓓ
2. Ⓐ Ⓑ Ⓒ Ⓓ
3. Ⓐ Ⓑ Ⓒ Ⓓ
4. Ⓐ Ⓑ Ⓒ Ⓓ
5. Ⓐ Ⓑ Ⓒ Ⓓ
6. Ⓐ Ⓑ Ⓒ Ⓓ
7. Ⓐ Ⓑ Ⓒ Ⓓ
8. Ⓐ Ⓑ Ⓒ Ⓓ
9. Ⓐ Ⓑ Ⓒ Ⓓ
10. Ⓐ Ⓑ Ⓒ Ⓓ

11. Ⓐ Ⓑ Ⓒ Ⓓ
12. Ⓐ Ⓑ Ⓒ Ⓓ
13. Ⓐ Ⓑ Ⓒ Ⓓ
14. Ⓐ Ⓑ Ⓒ Ⓓ
15. Ⓐ Ⓑ Ⓒ Ⓓ
16. Ⓐ Ⓑ Ⓒ Ⓓ
17. Ⓐ Ⓑ Ⓒ Ⓓ
18. Ⓐ Ⓑ Ⓒ Ⓓ
19. Ⓐ Ⓑ Ⓒ Ⓓ
20. Ⓐ Ⓑ Ⓒ Ⓓ

21. Ⓐ Ⓑ Ⓒ Ⓓ
22. Ⓐ Ⓑ Ⓒ Ⓓ
23. Ⓐ Ⓑ Ⓒ Ⓓ
24. Ⓐ Ⓑ Ⓒ Ⓓ
25. Ⓐ Ⓑ Ⓒ Ⓓ
26. Ⓐ Ⓑ Ⓒ Ⓓ
27. Ⓐ Ⓑ Ⓒ Ⓓ
28. Ⓐ Ⓑ Ⓒ Ⓓ
29. Ⓐ Ⓑ Ⓒ Ⓓ
30. Ⓐ Ⓑ Ⓒ Ⓓ

POSTAL EXAM 473/473c
ANSWER SHEET

PRACTICE TEST 1: CODING AND MEMORY

Section 1: Coding

1. Ⓐ Ⓑ Ⓒ Ⓓ
2. Ⓐ Ⓑ Ⓒ Ⓓ
3. Ⓐ Ⓑ Ⓒ Ⓓ
4. Ⓐ Ⓑ Ⓒ Ⓓ
5. Ⓐ Ⓑ Ⓒ Ⓓ
6. Ⓐ Ⓑ Ⓒ Ⓓ
7. Ⓐ Ⓑ Ⓒ Ⓓ
8. Ⓐ Ⓑ Ⓒ Ⓓ
9. Ⓐ Ⓑ Ⓒ Ⓓ
10. Ⓐ Ⓑ Ⓒ Ⓓ
11. Ⓐ Ⓑ Ⓒ Ⓓ
12. Ⓐ Ⓑ Ⓒ Ⓓ

13. Ⓐ Ⓑ Ⓒ Ⓓ
14. Ⓐ Ⓑ Ⓒ Ⓓ
15. Ⓐ Ⓑ Ⓒ Ⓓ
16. Ⓐ Ⓑ Ⓒ Ⓓ
17. Ⓐ Ⓑ Ⓒ Ⓓ
18. Ⓐ Ⓑ Ⓒ Ⓓ
19. Ⓐ Ⓑ Ⓒ Ⓓ
20. Ⓐ Ⓑ Ⓒ Ⓓ
21. Ⓐ Ⓑ Ⓒ Ⓓ
22. Ⓐ Ⓑ Ⓒ Ⓓ
23. Ⓐ Ⓑ Ⓒ Ⓓ
24. Ⓐ Ⓑ Ⓒ Ⓓ

25. Ⓐ Ⓑ Ⓒ Ⓓ
26. Ⓐ Ⓑ Ⓒ Ⓓ
27. Ⓐ Ⓑ Ⓒ Ⓓ
28. Ⓐ Ⓑ Ⓒ Ⓓ
29. Ⓐ Ⓑ Ⓒ Ⓓ
30. Ⓐ Ⓑ Ⓒ Ⓓ
31. Ⓐ Ⓑ Ⓒ Ⓓ
32. Ⓐ Ⓑ Ⓒ Ⓓ
33. Ⓐ Ⓑ Ⓒ Ⓓ
34. Ⓐ Ⓑ Ⓒ Ⓓ
35. Ⓐ Ⓑ Ⓒ Ⓓ
36. Ⓐ Ⓑ Ⓒ Ⓓ

POSTAL EXAM 473/473c
ANSWER SHEET

Section 2: Memory

1. Ⓐ Ⓑ Ⓒ Ⓓ	13. Ⓐ Ⓑ Ⓒ Ⓓ	25. Ⓐ Ⓑ Ⓒ Ⓓ
2. Ⓐ Ⓑ Ⓒ Ⓓ	14. Ⓐ Ⓑ Ⓒ Ⓓ	26. Ⓐ Ⓑ Ⓒ Ⓓ
3. Ⓐ Ⓑ Ⓒ Ⓓ	15. Ⓐ Ⓑ Ⓒ Ⓓ	27. Ⓐ Ⓑ Ⓒ Ⓓ
4. Ⓐ Ⓑ Ⓒ Ⓓ	16. Ⓐ Ⓑ Ⓒ Ⓓ	28. Ⓐ Ⓑ Ⓒ Ⓓ
5. Ⓐ Ⓑ Ⓒ Ⓓ	17. Ⓐ Ⓑ Ⓒ Ⓓ	29. Ⓐ Ⓑ Ⓒ Ⓓ
6. Ⓐ Ⓑ Ⓒ Ⓓ	18. Ⓐ Ⓑ Ⓒ Ⓓ	30. Ⓐ Ⓑ Ⓒ Ⓓ
7. Ⓐ Ⓑ Ⓒ Ⓓ	19. Ⓐ Ⓑ Ⓒ Ⓓ	31. Ⓐ Ⓑ Ⓒ Ⓓ
8. Ⓐ Ⓑ Ⓒ Ⓓ	20. Ⓐ Ⓑ Ⓒ Ⓓ	32. Ⓐ Ⓑ Ⓒ Ⓓ
9. Ⓐ Ⓑ Ⓒ Ⓓ	21. Ⓐ Ⓑ Ⓒ Ⓓ	33. Ⓐ Ⓑ Ⓒ Ⓓ
10. Ⓐ Ⓑ Ⓒ Ⓓ	22. Ⓐ Ⓑ Ⓒ Ⓓ	34. Ⓐ Ⓑ Ⓒ Ⓓ
11. Ⓐ Ⓑ Ⓒ Ⓓ	23. Ⓐ Ⓑ Ⓒ Ⓓ	35. Ⓐ Ⓑ Ⓒ Ⓓ
12. Ⓐ Ⓑ Ⓒ Ⓓ	24. Ⓐ Ⓑ Ⓒ Ⓓ	36. Ⓐ Ⓑ Ⓒ Ⓓ

POSTAL EXAM 473/473c
ANSWER SHEET

PRACTICE TEST 2: ADDRESS CHECKING

1. Ⓐ Ⓑ Ⓒ Ⓓ	21. Ⓐ Ⓑ Ⓒ Ⓓ	41. Ⓐ Ⓑ Ⓒ Ⓓ
2. Ⓐ Ⓑ Ⓒ Ⓓ	22. Ⓐ Ⓑ Ⓒ Ⓓ	42. Ⓐ Ⓑ Ⓒ Ⓓ
3. Ⓐ Ⓑ Ⓒ Ⓓ	23. Ⓐ Ⓑ Ⓒ Ⓓ	43. Ⓐ Ⓑ Ⓒ Ⓓ
4. Ⓐ Ⓑ Ⓒ Ⓓ	24. Ⓐ Ⓑ Ⓒ Ⓓ	44. Ⓐ Ⓑ Ⓒ Ⓓ
5. Ⓐ Ⓑ Ⓒ Ⓓ	25. Ⓐ Ⓑ Ⓒ Ⓓ	45. Ⓐ Ⓑ Ⓒ Ⓓ
6. Ⓐ Ⓑ Ⓒ Ⓓ	26. Ⓐ Ⓑ Ⓒ Ⓓ	46. Ⓐ Ⓑ Ⓒ Ⓓ
7. Ⓐ Ⓑ Ⓒ Ⓓ	27. Ⓐ Ⓑ Ⓒ Ⓓ	47. Ⓐ Ⓑ Ⓒ Ⓓ
8. Ⓐ Ⓑ Ⓒ Ⓓ	28. Ⓐ Ⓑ Ⓒ Ⓓ	48. Ⓐ Ⓑ Ⓒ Ⓓ
9. Ⓐ Ⓑ Ⓒ Ⓓ	29. Ⓐ Ⓑ Ⓒ Ⓓ	49. Ⓐ Ⓑ Ⓒ Ⓓ
10. Ⓐ Ⓑ Ⓒ Ⓓ	30. Ⓐ Ⓑ Ⓒ Ⓓ	50. Ⓐ Ⓑ Ⓒ Ⓓ
11. Ⓐ Ⓑ Ⓒ Ⓓ	31. Ⓐ Ⓑ Ⓒ Ⓓ	51. Ⓐ Ⓑ Ⓒ Ⓓ
12. Ⓐ Ⓑ Ⓒ Ⓓ	32. Ⓐ Ⓑ Ⓒ Ⓓ	52. Ⓐ Ⓑ Ⓒ Ⓓ
13. Ⓐ Ⓑ Ⓒ Ⓓ	33. Ⓐ Ⓑ Ⓒ Ⓓ	53. Ⓐ Ⓑ Ⓒ Ⓓ
14. Ⓐ Ⓑ Ⓒ Ⓓ	34. Ⓐ Ⓑ Ⓒ Ⓓ	54. Ⓐ Ⓑ Ⓒ Ⓓ
15. Ⓐ Ⓑ Ⓒ Ⓓ	35. Ⓐ Ⓑ Ⓒ Ⓓ	55. Ⓐ Ⓑ Ⓒ Ⓓ
16. Ⓐ Ⓑ Ⓒ Ⓓ	36. Ⓐ Ⓑ Ⓒ Ⓓ	56. Ⓐ Ⓑ Ⓒ Ⓓ
17. Ⓐ Ⓑ Ⓒ Ⓓ	37. Ⓐ Ⓑ Ⓒ Ⓓ	57. Ⓐ Ⓑ Ⓒ Ⓓ
18. Ⓐ Ⓑ Ⓒ Ⓓ	38. Ⓐ Ⓑ Ⓒ Ⓓ	58. Ⓐ Ⓑ Ⓒ Ⓓ
19. Ⓐ Ⓑ Ⓒ Ⓓ	39. Ⓐ Ⓑ Ⓒ Ⓓ	59. Ⓐ Ⓑ Ⓒ Ⓓ
20. Ⓐ Ⓑ Ⓒ Ⓓ	40. Ⓐ Ⓑ Ⓒ Ⓓ	60. Ⓐ Ⓑ Ⓒ Ⓓ

POSTAL EXAM 473/473c
ANSWER SHEET

PRACTICE TEST 2: FORMS COMPLETION

1. Ⓐ Ⓑ Ⓒ Ⓓ
2. Ⓐ Ⓑ Ⓒ Ⓓ
3. Ⓐ Ⓑ Ⓒ Ⓓ
4. Ⓐ Ⓑ Ⓒ Ⓓ
5. Ⓐ Ⓑ Ⓒ Ⓓ
6. Ⓐ Ⓑ Ⓒ Ⓓ
7. Ⓐ Ⓑ Ⓒ Ⓓ
8. Ⓐ Ⓑ Ⓒ Ⓓ
9. Ⓐ Ⓑ Ⓒ Ⓓ
10. Ⓐ Ⓑ Ⓒ Ⓓ

11. Ⓐ Ⓑ Ⓒ Ⓓ
12. Ⓐ Ⓑ Ⓒ Ⓓ
13. Ⓐ Ⓑ Ⓒ Ⓓ
14. Ⓐ Ⓑ Ⓒ Ⓓ
15. Ⓐ Ⓑ Ⓒ Ⓓ
16. Ⓐ Ⓑ Ⓒ Ⓓ
17. Ⓐ Ⓑ Ⓒ Ⓓ
18. Ⓐ Ⓑ Ⓒ Ⓓ
19. Ⓐ Ⓑ Ⓒ Ⓓ
20. Ⓐ Ⓑ Ⓒ Ⓓ

21. Ⓐ Ⓑ Ⓒ Ⓓ
22. Ⓐ Ⓑ Ⓒ Ⓓ
23. Ⓐ Ⓑ Ⓒ Ⓓ
24. Ⓐ Ⓑ Ⓒ Ⓓ
25. Ⓐ Ⓑ Ⓒ Ⓓ
26. Ⓐ Ⓑ Ⓒ Ⓓ
27. Ⓐ Ⓑ Ⓒ Ⓓ
28. Ⓐ Ⓑ Ⓒ Ⓓ
29. Ⓐ Ⓑ Ⓒ Ⓓ
30. Ⓐ Ⓑ Ⓒ Ⓓ

POSTAL EXAM 473/473c
ANSWER SHEET

PRACTICE TEST 2: CODING AND MEMORY

Section 1: Coding

1. Ⓐ Ⓑ Ⓒ Ⓓ
2. Ⓐ Ⓑ Ⓒ Ⓓ
3. Ⓐ Ⓑ Ⓒ Ⓓ
4. Ⓐ Ⓑ Ⓒ Ⓓ
5. Ⓐ Ⓑ Ⓒ Ⓓ
6. Ⓐ Ⓑ Ⓒ Ⓓ
7. Ⓐ Ⓑ Ⓒ Ⓓ
8. Ⓐ Ⓑ Ⓒ Ⓓ
9. Ⓐ Ⓑ Ⓒ Ⓓ
10. Ⓐ Ⓑ Ⓒ Ⓓ
11. Ⓐ Ⓑ Ⓒ Ⓓ
12. Ⓐ Ⓑ Ⓒ Ⓓ

13. Ⓐ Ⓑ Ⓒ Ⓓ
14. Ⓐ Ⓑ Ⓒ Ⓓ
15. Ⓐ Ⓑ Ⓒ Ⓓ
16. Ⓐ Ⓑ Ⓒ Ⓓ
17. Ⓐ Ⓑ Ⓒ Ⓓ
18. Ⓐ Ⓑ Ⓒ Ⓓ
19. Ⓐ Ⓑ Ⓒ Ⓓ
20. Ⓐ Ⓑ Ⓒ Ⓓ
21. Ⓐ Ⓑ Ⓒ Ⓓ
22. Ⓐ Ⓑ Ⓒ Ⓓ
23. Ⓐ Ⓑ Ⓒ Ⓓ
24. Ⓐ Ⓑ Ⓒ Ⓓ

25. Ⓐ Ⓑ Ⓒ Ⓓ
26. Ⓐ Ⓑ Ⓒ Ⓓ
27. Ⓐ Ⓑ Ⓒ Ⓓ
28. Ⓐ Ⓑ Ⓒ Ⓓ
29. Ⓐ Ⓑ Ⓒ Ⓓ
30. Ⓐ Ⓑ Ⓒ Ⓓ
31. Ⓐ Ⓑ Ⓒ Ⓓ
32. Ⓐ Ⓑ Ⓒ Ⓓ
33. Ⓐ Ⓑ Ⓒ Ⓓ
34. Ⓐ Ⓑ Ⓒ Ⓓ
35. Ⓐ Ⓑ Ⓒ Ⓓ
36. Ⓐ Ⓑ Ⓒ Ⓓ

POSTAL EXAM 473/473c
ANSWER SHEET

Section 2: Memory

1. Ⓐ Ⓑ Ⓒ Ⓓ
2. Ⓐ Ⓑ Ⓒ Ⓓ
3. Ⓐ Ⓑ Ⓒ Ⓓ
4. Ⓐ Ⓑ Ⓒ Ⓓ
5. Ⓐ Ⓑ Ⓒ Ⓓ
6. Ⓐ Ⓑ Ⓒ Ⓓ
7. Ⓐ Ⓑ Ⓒ Ⓓ
8. Ⓐ Ⓑ Ⓒ Ⓓ
9. Ⓐ Ⓑ Ⓒ Ⓓ
10. Ⓐ Ⓑ Ⓒ Ⓓ
11. Ⓐ Ⓑ Ⓒ Ⓓ
12. Ⓐ Ⓑ Ⓒ Ⓓ

13. Ⓐ Ⓑ Ⓒ Ⓓ
14. Ⓐ Ⓑ Ⓒ Ⓓ
15. Ⓐ Ⓑ Ⓒ Ⓓ
16. Ⓐ Ⓑ Ⓒ Ⓓ
17. Ⓐ Ⓑ Ⓒ Ⓓ
18. Ⓐ Ⓑ Ⓒ Ⓓ
19. Ⓐ Ⓑ Ⓒ Ⓓ
20. Ⓐ Ⓑ Ⓒ Ⓓ
21. Ⓐ Ⓑ Ⓒ Ⓓ
22. Ⓐ Ⓑ Ⓒ Ⓓ
23. Ⓐ Ⓑ Ⓒ Ⓓ
24. Ⓐ Ⓑ Ⓒ Ⓓ

25. Ⓐ Ⓑ Ⓒ Ⓓ
26. Ⓐ Ⓑ Ⓒ Ⓓ
27. Ⓐ Ⓑ Ⓒ Ⓓ
28. Ⓐ Ⓑ Ⓒ Ⓓ
29. Ⓐ Ⓑ Ⓒ Ⓓ
30. Ⓐ Ⓑ Ⓒ Ⓓ
31. Ⓐ Ⓑ Ⓒ Ⓓ
32. Ⓐ Ⓑ Ⓒ Ⓓ
33. Ⓐ Ⓑ Ⓒ Ⓓ
34. Ⓐ Ⓑ Ⓒ Ⓓ
35. Ⓐ Ⓑ Ⓒ Ⓓ
36. Ⓐ Ⓑ Ⓒ Ⓓ

POSTAL EXAM 473/473c
ANSWER SHEET

PRACTICE TEST 3: ADDRESS CHECKING

1. Ⓐ Ⓑ Ⓒ Ⓓ
2. Ⓐ Ⓑ Ⓒ Ⓓ
3. Ⓐ Ⓑ Ⓒ Ⓓ
4. Ⓐ Ⓑ Ⓒ Ⓓ
5. Ⓐ Ⓑ Ⓒ Ⓓ
6. Ⓐ Ⓑ Ⓒ Ⓓ
7. Ⓐ Ⓑ Ⓒ Ⓓ
8. Ⓐ Ⓑ Ⓒ Ⓓ
9. Ⓐ Ⓑ Ⓒ Ⓓ
10. Ⓐ Ⓑ Ⓒ Ⓓ
11. Ⓐ Ⓑ Ⓒ Ⓓ
12. Ⓐ Ⓑ Ⓒ Ⓓ
13. Ⓐ Ⓑ Ⓒ Ⓓ
14. Ⓐ Ⓑ Ⓒ Ⓓ
15. Ⓐ Ⓑ Ⓒ Ⓓ
16. Ⓐ Ⓑ Ⓒ Ⓓ
17. Ⓐ Ⓑ Ⓒ Ⓓ
18. Ⓐ Ⓑ Ⓒ Ⓓ
19. Ⓐ Ⓑ Ⓒ Ⓓ
20. Ⓐ Ⓑ Ⓒ Ⓓ

21. Ⓐ Ⓑ Ⓒ Ⓓ
22. Ⓐ Ⓑ Ⓒ Ⓓ
23. Ⓐ Ⓑ Ⓒ Ⓓ
24. Ⓐ Ⓑ Ⓒ Ⓓ
25. Ⓐ Ⓑ Ⓒ Ⓓ
26. Ⓐ Ⓑ Ⓒ Ⓓ
27. Ⓐ Ⓑ Ⓒ Ⓓ
28. Ⓐ Ⓑ Ⓒ Ⓓ
29. Ⓐ Ⓑ Ⓒ Ⓓ
30. Ⓐ Ⓑ Ⓒ Ⓓ
31. Ⓐ Ⓑ Ⓒ Ⓓ
32. Ⓐ Ⓑ Ⓒ Ⓓ
33. Ⓐ Ⓑ Ⓒ Ⓓ
34. Ⓐ Ⓑ Ⓒ Ⓓ
35. Ⓐ Ⓑ Ⓒ Ⓓ
36. Ⓐ Ⓑ Ⓒ Ⓓ
37. Ⓐ Ⓑ Ⓒ Ⓓ
38. Ⓐ Ⓑ Ⓒ Ⓓ
39. Ⓐ Ⓑ Ⓒ Ⓓ
40. Ⓐ Ⓑ Ⓒ Ⓓ

41. Ⓐ Ⓑ Ⓒ Ⓓ
42. Ⓐ Ⓑ Ⓒ Ⓓ
43. Ⓐ Ⓑ Ⓒ Ⓓ
44. Ⓐ Ⓑ Ⓒ Ⓓ
45. Ⓐ Ⓑ Ⓒ Ⓓ
46. Ⓐ Ⓑ Ⓒ Ⓓ
47. Ⓐ Ⓑ Ⓒ Ⓓ
48. Ⓐ Ⓑ Ⓒ Ⓓ
49. Ⓐ Ⓑ Ⓒ Ⓓ
50. Ⓐ Ⓑ Ⓒ Ⓓ
51. Ⓐ Ⓑ Ⓒ Ⓓ
52. Ⓐ Ⓑ Ⓒ Ⓓ
53. Ⓐ Ⓑ Ⓒ Ⓓ
54. Ⓐ Ⓑ Ⓒ Ⓓ
55. Ⓐ Ⓑ Ⓒ Ⓓ
56. Ⓐ Ⓑ Ⓒ Ⓓ
57. Ⓐ Ⓑ Ⓒ Ⓓ
58. Ⓐ Ⓑ Ⓒ Ⓓ
59. Ⓐ Ⓑ Ⓒ Ⓓ
60. Ⓐ Ⓑ Ⓒ Ⓓ

POSTAL EXAM 473/473c
ANSWER SHEET

PRACTICE TEST 3: FORMS COMPLETION

1. Ⓐ Ⓑ Ⓒ Ⓓ	11. Ⓐ Ⓑ Ⓒ Ⓓ	21. Ⓐ Ⓑ Ⓒ Ⓓ
2. Ⓐ Ⓑ Ⓒ Ⓓ	12. Ⓐ Ⓑ Ⓒ Ⓓ	22. Ⓐ Ⓑ Ⓒ Ⓓ
3. Ⓐ Ⓑ Ⓒ Ⓓ	13. Ⓐ Ⓑ Ⓒ Ⓓ	23. Ⓐ Ⓑ Ⓒ Ⓓ
4. Ⓐ Ⓑ Ⓒ Ⓓ	14. Ⓐ Ⓑ Ⓒ Ⓓ	24. Ⓐ Ⓑ Ⓒ Ⓓ
5. Ⓐ Ⓑ Ⓒ Ⓓ	15. Ⓐ Ⓑ Ⓒ Ⓓ	25. Ⓐ Ⓑ Ⓒ Ⓓ
6. Ⓐ Ⓑ Ⓒ Ⓓ	16. Ⓐ Ⓑ Ⓒ Ⓓ	26. Ⓐ Ⓑ Ⓒ Ⓓ
7. Ⓐ Ⓑ Ⓒ Ⓓ	17. Ⓐ Ⓑ Ⓒ Ⓓ	27. Ⓐ Ⓑ Ⓒ Ⓓ
8. Ⓐ Ⓑ Ⓒ Ⓓ	18. Ⓐ Ⓑ Ⓒ Ⓓ	28. Ⓐ Ⓑ Ⓒ Ⓓ
9. Ⓐ Ⓑ Ⓒ Ⓓ	19. Ⓐ Ⓑ Ⓒ Ⓓ	29. Ⓐ Ⓑ Ⓒ Ⓓ
10. Ⓐ Ⓑ Ⓒ Ⓓ	20. Ⓐ Ⓑ Ⓒ Ⓓ	30. Ⓐ Ⓑ Ⓒ Ⓓ

POSTAL EXAM 473/473c
ANSWER SHEET

PRACTICE TEST 3: CODING AND MEMORY

Section 1: Coding

1. Ⓐ Ⓑ Ⓒ Ⓓ
2. Ⓐ Ⓑ Ⓒ Ⓓ
3. Ⓐ Ⓑ Ⓒ Ⓓ
4. Ⓐ Ⓑ Ⓒ Ⓓ
5. Ⓐ Ⓑ Ⓒ Ⓓ
6. Ⓐ Ⓑ Ⓒ Ⓓ
7. Ⓐ Ⓑ Ⓒ Ⓓ
8. Ⓐ Ⓑ Ⓒ Ⓓ
9. Ⓐ Ⓑ Ⓒ Ⓓ
10. Ⓐ Ⓑ Ⓒ Ⓓ
11. Ⓐ Ⓑ Ⓒ Ⓓ
12. Ⓐ Ⓑ Ⓒ Ⓓ

13. Ⓐ Ⓑ Ⓒ Ⓓ
14. Ⓐ Ⓑ Ⓒ Ⓓ
15. Ⓐ Ⓑ Ⓒ Ⓓ
16. Ⓐ Ⓑ Ⓒ Ⓓ
17. Ⓐ Ⓑ Ⓒ Ⓓ
18. Ⓐ Ⓑ Ⓒ Ⓓ
19. Ⓐ Ⓑ Ⓒ Ⓓ
20. Ⓐ Ⓑ Ⓒ Ⓓ
21. Ⓐ Ⓑ Ⓒ Ⓓ
22. Ⓐ Ⓑ Ⓒ Ⓓ
23. Ⓐ Ⓑ Ⓒ Ⓓ
24. Ⓐ Ⓑ Ⓒ Ⓓ

25. Ⓐ Ⓑ Ⓒ Ⓓ
26. Ⓐ Ⓑ Ⓒ Ⓓ
27. Ⓐ Ⓑ Ⓒ Ⓓ
28. Ⓐ Ⓑ Ⓒ Ⓓ
29. Ⓐ Ⓑ Ⓒ Ⓓ
30. Ⓐ Ⓑ Ⓒ Ⓓ
31. Ⓐ Ⓑ Ⓒ Ⓓ
32. Ⓐ Ⓑ Ⓒ Ⓓ
33. Ⓐ Ⓑ Ⓒ Ⓓ
34. Ⓐ Ⓑ Ⓒ Ⓓ
35. Ⓐ Ⓑ Ⓒ Ⓓ
36. Ⓐ Ⓑ Ⓒ Ⓓ

POSTAL EXAM 473/473c
ANSWER SHEET

Section 2: Memory

1. Ⓐ Ⓑ Ⓒ Ⓓ
2. Ⓐ Ⓑ Ⓒ Ⓓ
3. Ⓐ Ⓑ Ⓒ Ⓓ
4. Ⓐ Ⓑ Ⓒ Ⓓ
5. Ⓐ Ⓑ Ⓒ Ⓓ
6. Ⓐ Ⓑ Ⓒ Ⓓ
7. Ⓐ Ⓑ Ⓒ Ⓓ
8. Ⓐ Ⓑ Ⓒ Ⓓ
9. Ⓐ Ⓑ Ⓒ Ⓓ
10. Ⓐ Ⓑ Ⓒ Ⓓ
11. Ⓐ Ⓑ Ⓒ Ⓓ
12. Ⓐ Ⓑ Ⓒ Ⓓ

13. Ⓐ Ⓑ Ⓒ Ⓓ
14. Ⓐ Ⓑ Ⓒ Ⓓ
15. Ⓐ Ⓑ Ⓒ Ⓓ
16. Ⓐ Ⓑ Ⓒ Ⓓ
17. Ⓐ Ⓑ Ⓒ Ⓓ
18. Ⓐ Ⓑ Ⓒ Ⓓ
19. Ⓐ Ⓑ Ⓒ Ⓓ
20. Ⓐ Ⓑ Ⓒ Ⓓ
21. Ⓐ Ⓑ Ⓒ Ⓓ
22. Ⓐ Ⓑ Ⓒ Ⓓ
23. Ⓐ Ⓑ Ⓒ Ⓓ
24. Ⓐ Ⓑ Ⓒ Ⓓ

25. Ⓐ Ⓑ Ⓒ Ⓓ
26. Ⓐ Ⓑ Ⓒ Ⓓ
27. Ⓐ Ⓑ Ⓒ Ⓓ
28. Ⓐ Ⓑ Ⓒ Ⓓ
29. Ⓐ Ⓑ Ⓒ Ⓓ
30. Ⓐ Ⓑ Ⓒ Ⓓ
31. Ⓐ Ⓑ Ⓒ Ⓓ
32. Ⓐ Ⓑ Ⓒ Ⓓ
33. Ⓐ Ⓑ Ⓒ Ⓓ
34. Ⓐ Ⓑ Ⓒ Ⓓ
35. Ⓐ Ⓑ Ⓒ Ⓓ
36. Ⓐ Ⓑ Ⓒ Ⓓ

POSTAL EXAM 473/473c
ANSWER SHEET

PRACTICE TEST 4: ADDRESS CHECKING

1. Ⓐ Ⓑ Ⓒ Ⓓ
2. Ⓐ Ⓑ Ⓒ Ⓓ
3. Ⓐ Ⓑ Ⓒ Ⓓ
4. Ⓐ Ⓑ Ⓒ Ⓓ
5. Ⓐ Ⓑ Ⓒ Ⓓ
6. Ⓐ Ⓑ Ⓒ Ⓓ
7. Ⓐ Ⓑ Ⓒ Ⓓ
8. Ⓐ Ⓑ Ⓒ Ⓓ
9. Ⓐ Ⓑ Ⓒ Ⓓ
10. Ⓐ Ⓑ Ⓒ Ⓓ
11. Ⓐ Ⓑ Ⓒ Ⓓ
12. Ⓐ Ⓑ Ⓒ Ⓓ
13. Ⓐ Ⓑ Ⓒ Ⓓ
14. Ⓐ Ⓑ Ⓒ Ⓓ
15. Ⓐ Ⓑ Ⓒ Ⓓ
16. Ⓐ Ⓑ Ⓒ Ⓓ
17. Ⓐ Ⓑ Ⓒ Ⓓ
18. Ⓐ Ⓑ Ⓒ Ⓓ
19. Ⓐ Ⓑ Ⓒ Ⓓ
20. Ⓐ Ⓑ Ⓒ Ⓓ

21. Ⓐ Ⓑ Ⓒ Ⓓ
22. Ⓐ Ⓑ Ⓒ Ⓓ
23. Ⓐ Ⓑ Ⓒ Ⓓ
24. Ⓐ Ⓑ Ⓒ Ⓓ
25. Ⓐ Ⓑ Ⓒ Ⓓ
26. Ⓐ Ⓑ Ⓒ Ⓓ
27. Ⓐ Ⓑ Ⓒ Ⓓ
28. Ⓐ Ⓑ Ⓒ Ⓓ
29. Ⓐ Ⓑ Ⓒ Ⓓ
30. Ⓐ Ⓑ Ⓒ Ⓓ
31. Ⓐ Ⓑ Ⓒ Ⓓ
32. Ⓐ Ⓑ Ⓒ Ⓓ
33. Ⓐ Ⓑ Ⓒ Ⓓ
34. Ⓐ Ⓑ Ⓒ Ⓓ
35. Ⓐ Ⓑ Ⓒ Ⓓ
36. Ⓐ Ⓑ Ⓒ Ⓓ
37. Ⓐ Ⓑ Ⓒ Ⓓ
38. Ⓐ Ⓑ Ⓒ Ⓓ
39. Ⓐ Ⓑ Ⓒ Ⓓ
40. Ⓐ Ⓑ Ⓒ Ⓓ

41. Ⓐ Ⓑ Ⓒ Ⓓ
42. Ⓐ Ⓑ Ⓒ Ⓓ
43. Ⓐ Ⓑ Ⓒ Ⓓ
44. Ⓐ Ⓑ Ⓒ Ⓓ
45. Ⓐ Ⓑ Ⓒ Ⓓ
46. Ⓐ Ⓑ Ⓒ Ⓓ
47. Ⓐ Ⓑ Ⓒ Ⓓ
48. Ⓐ Ⓑ Ⓒ Ⓓ
49. Ⓐ Ⓑ Ⓒ Ⓓ
50. Ⓐ Ⓑ Ⓒ Ⓓ
51. Ⓐ Ⓑ Ⓒ Ⓓ
52. Ⓐ Ⓑ Ⓒ Ⓓ
53. Ⓐ Ⓑ Ⓒ Ⓓ
54. Ⓐ Ⓑ Ⓒ Ⓓ
55. Ⓐ Ⓑ Ⓒ Ⓓ
56. Ⓐ Ⓑ Ⓒ Ⓓ
57. Ⓐ Ⓑ Ⓒ Ⓓ
58. Ⓐ Ⓑ Ⓒ Ⓓ
59. Ⓐ Ⓑ Ⓒ Ⓓ
60. Ⓐ Ⓑ Ⓒ Ⓓ

POSTAL EXAM 473/473c
ANSWER SHEET

PRACTICE TEST 4: FORMS COMPLETION

1. Ⓐ Ⓑ Ⓒ Ⓓ
2. Ⓐ Ⓑ Ⓒ Ⓓ
3. Ⓐ Ⓑ Ⓒ Ⓓ
4. Ⓐ Ⓑ Ⓒ Ⓓ
5. Ⓐ Ⓑ Ⓒ Ⓓ
6. Ⓐ Ⓑ Ⓒ Ⓓ
7. Ⓐ Ⓑ Ⓒ Ⓓ
8. Ⓐ Ⓑ Ⓒ Ⓓ
9. Ⓐ Ⓑ Ⓒ Ⓓ
10. Ⓐ Ⓑ Ⓒ Ⓓ

11. Ⓐ Ⓑ Ⓒ Ⓓ
12. Ⓐ Ⓑ Ⓒ Ⓓ
13. Ⓐ Ⓑ Ⓒ Ⓓ
14. Ⓐ Ⓑ Ⓒ Ⓓ
15. Ⓐ Ⓑ Ⓒ Ⓓ
16. Ⓐ Ⓑ Ⓒ Ⓓ
17. Ⓐ Ⓑ Ⓒ Ⓓ
18. Ⓐ Ⓑ Ⓒ Ⓓ
19. Ⓐ Ⓑ Ⓒ Ⓓ
20. Ⓐ Ⓑ Ⓒ Ⓓ

21. Ⓐ Ⓑ Ⓒ Ⓓ
22. Ⓐ Ⓑ Ⓒ Ⓓ
23. Ⓐ Ⓑ Ⓒ Ⓓ
24. Ⓐ Ⓑ Ⓒ Ⓓ
25. Ⓐ Ⓑ Ⓒ Ⓓ
26. Ⓐ Ⓑ Ⓒ Ⓓ
27. Ⓐ Ⓑ Ⓒ Ⓓ
28. Ⓐ Ⓑ Ⓒ Ⓓ
29. Ⓐ Ⓑ Ⓒ Ⓓ
30. Ⓐ Ⓑ Ⓒ Ⓓ

POSTAL EXAM 473/473c
ANSWER SHEET

PRACTICE TEST 4: CODING AND MEMORY

Section 1: Coding

1. Ⓐ Ⓑ Ⓒ Ⓓ
2. Ⓐ Ⓑ Ⓒ Ⓓ
3. Ⓐ Ⓑ Ⓒ Ⓓ
4. Ⓐ Ⓑ Ⓒ Ⓓ
5. Ⓐ Ⓑ Ⓒ Ⓓ
6. Ⓐ Ⓑ Ⓒ Ⓓ
7. Ⓐ Ⓑ Ⓒ Ⓓ
8. Ⓐ Ⓑ Ⓒ Ⓓ
9. Ⓐ Ⓑ Ⓒ Ⓓ
10. Ⓐ Ⓑ Ⓒ Ⓓ
11. Ⓐ Ⓑ Ⓒ Ⓓ
12. Ⓐ Ⓑ Ⓒ Ⓓ

13. Ⓐ Ⓑ Ⓒ Ⓓ
14. Ⓐ Ⓑ Ⓒ Ⓓ
15. Ⓐ Ⓑ Ⓒ Ⓓ
16. Ⓐ Ⓑ Ⓒ Ⓓ
17. Ⓐ Ⓑ Ⓒ Ⓓ
18. Ⓐ Ⓑ Ⓒ Ⓓ
19. Ⓐ Ⓑ Ⓒ Ⓓ
20. Ⓐ Ⓑ Ⓒ Ⓓ
21. Ⓐ Ⓑ Ⓒ Ⓓ
22. Ⓐ Ⓑ Ⓒ Ⓓ
23. Ⓐ Ⓑ Ⓒ Ⓓ
24. Ⓐ Ⓑ Ⓒ Ⓓ

25. Ⓐ Ⓑ Ⓒ Ⓓ
26. Ⓐ Ⓑ Ⓒ Ⓓ
27. Ⓐ Ⓑ Ⓒ Ⓓ
28. Ⓐ Ⓑ Ⓒ Ⓓ
29. Ⓐ Ⓑ Ⓒ Ⓓ
30. Ⓐ Ⓑ Ⓒ Ⓓ
31. Ⓐ Ⓑ Ⓒ Ⓓ
32. Ⓐ Ⓑ Ⓒ Ⓓ
33. Ⓐ Ⓑ Ⓒ Ⓓ
34. Ⓐ Ⓑ Ⓒ Ⓓ
35. Ⓐ Ⓑ Ⓒ Ⓓ
36. Ⓐ Ⓑ Ⓒ Ⓓ

POSTAL EXAM 473/473c
ANSWER SHEET

Section 2: Memory

1. Ⓐ Ⓑ Ⓒ Ⓓ
2. Ⓐ Ⓑ Ⓒ Ⓓ
3. Ⓐ Ⓑ Ⓒ Ⓓ
4. Ⓐ Ⓑ Ⓒ Ⓓ
5. Ⓐ Ⓑ Ⓒ Ⓓ
6. Ⓐ Ⓑ Ⓒ Ⓓ
7. Ⓐ Ⓑ Ⓒ Ⓓ
8. Ⓐ Ⓑ Ⓒ Ⓓ
9. Ⓐ Ⓑ Ⓒ Ⓓ
10. Ⓐ Ⓑ Ⓒ Ⓓ
11. Ⓐ Ⓑ Ⓒ Ⓓ
12. Ⓐ Ⓑ Ⓒ Ⓓ

13. Ⓐ Ⓑ Ⓒ Ⓓ
14. Ⓐ Ⓑ Ⓒ Ⓓ
15. Ⓐ Ⓑ Ⓒ Ⓓ
16. Ⓐ Ⓑ Ⓒ Ⓓ
17. Ⓐ Ⓑ Ⓒ Ⓓ
18. Ⓐ Ⓑ Ⓒ Ⓓ
19. Ⓐ Ⓑ Ⓒ Ⓓ
20. Ⓐ Ⓑ Ⓒ Ⓓ
21. Ⓐ Ⓑ Ⓒ Ⓓ
22. Ⓐ Ⓑ Ⓒ Ⓓ
23. Ⓐ Ⓑ Ⓒ Ⓓ
24. Ⓐ Ⓑ Ⓒ Ⓓ

25. Ⓐ Ⓑ Ⓒ Ⓓ
26. Ⓐ Ⓑ Ⓒ Ⓓ
27. Ⓐ Ⓑ Ⓒ Ⓓ
28. Ⓐ Ⓑ Ⓒ Ⓓ
29. Ⓐ Ⓑ Ⓒ Ⓓ
30. Ⓐ Ⓑ Ⓒ Ⓓ
31. Ⓐ Ⓑ Ⓒ Ⓓ
32. Ⓐ Ⓑ Ⓒ Ⓓ
33. Ⓐ Ⓑ Ⓒ Ⓓ
34. Ⓐ Ⓑ Ⓒ Ⓓ
35. Ⓐ Ⓑ Ⓒ Ⓓ
36. Ⓐ Ⓑ Ⓒ Ⓓ

POSTAL EXAM 473/473c
ANSWER SHEET

PRACTICE TEST 5: ADDRESS CHECKING

1. Ⓐ Ⓑ Ⓒ Ⓓ	21. Ⓐ Ⓑ Ⓒ Ⓓ	41. Ⓐ Ⓑ Ⓒ Ⓓ
2. Ⓐ Ⓑ Ⓒ Ⓓ	22. Ⓐ Ⓑ Ⓒ Ⓓ	42. Ⓐ Ⓑ Ⓒ Ⓓ
3. Ⓐ Ⓑ Ⓒ Ⓓ	23. Ⓐ Ⓑ Ⓒ Ⓓ	43. Ⓐ Ⓑ Ⓒ Ⓓ
4. Ⓐ Ⓑ Ⓒ Ⓓ	24. Ⓐ Ⓑ Ⓒ Ⓓ	44. Ⓐ Ⓑ Ⓒ Ⓓ
5. Ⓐ Ⓑ Ⓒ Ⓓ	25. Ⓐ Ⓑ Ⓒ Ⓓ	45. Ⓐ Ⓑ Ⓒ Ⓓ
6. Ⓐ Ⓑ Ⓒ Ⓓ	26. Ⓐ Ⓑ Ⓒ Ⓓ	46. Ⓐ Ⓑ Ⓒ Ⓓ
7. Ⓐ Ⓑ Ⓒ Ⓓ	27. Ⓐ Ⓑ Ⓒ Ⓓ	47. Ⓐ Ⓑ Ⓒ Ⓓ
8. Ⓐ Ⓑ Ⓒ Ⓓ	28. Ⓐ Ⓑ Ⓒ Ⓓ	48. Ⓐ Ⓑ Ⓒ Ⓓ
9. Ⓐ Ⓑ Ⓒ Ⓓ	29. Ⓐ Ⓑ Ⓒ Ⓓ	49. Ⓐ Ⓑ Ⓒ Ⓓ
10. Ⓐ Ⓑ Ⓒ Ⓓ	30. Ⓐ Ⓑ Ⓒ Ⓓ	50. Ⓐ Ⓑ Ⓒ Ⓓ
11. Ⓐ Ⓑ Ⓒ Ⓓ	31. Ⓐ Ⓑ Ⓒ Ⓓ	51. Ⓐ Ⓑ Ⓒ Ⓓ
12. Ⓐ Ⓑ Ⓒ Ⓓ	32. Ⓐ Ⓑ Ⓒ Ⓓ	52. Ⓐ Ⓑ Ⓒ Ⓓ
13. Ⓐ Ⓑ Ⓒ Ⓓ	33. Ⓐ Ⓑ Ⓒ Ⓓ	53. Ⓐ Ⓑ Ⓒ Ⓓ
14. Ⓐ Ⓑ Ⓒ Ⓓ	34. Ⓐ Ⓑ Ⓒ Ⓓ	54. Ⓐ Ⓑ Ⓒ Ⓓ
15. Ⓐ Ⓑ Ⓒ Ⓓ	35. Ⓐ Ⓑ Ⓒ Ⓓ	55. Ⓐ Ⓑ Ⓒ Ⓓ
16. Ⓐ Ⓑ Ⓒ Ⓓ	36. Ⓐ Ⓑ Ⓒ Ⓓ	56. Ⓐ Ⓑ Ⓒ Ⓓ
17. Ⓐ Ⓑ Ⓒ Ⓓ	37. Ⓐ Ⓑ Ⓒ Ⓓ	57. Ⓐ Ⓑ Ⓒ Ⓓ
18. Ⓐ Ⓑ Ⓒ Ⓓ	38. Ⓐ Ⓑ Ⓒ Ⓓ	58. Ⓐ Ⓑ Ⓒ Ⓓ
19. Ⓐ Ⓑ Ⓒ Ⓓ	39. Ⓐ Ⓑ Ⓒ Ⓓ	59. Ⓐ Ⓑ Ⓒ Ⓓ
20. Ⓐ Ⓑ Ⓒ Ⓓ	40. Ⓐ Ⓑ Ⓒ Ⓓ	60. Ⓐ Ⓑ Ⓒ Ⓓ

POSTAL EXAM 473/473c
ANSWER SHEET

PRACTICE TEST 5: FORMS COMPLETION

1. Ⓐ Ⓑ Ⓒ Ⓓ
2. Ⓐ Ⓑ Ⓒ Ⓓ
3. Ⓐ Ⓑ Ⓒ Ⓓ
4. Ⓐ Ⓑ Ⓒ Ⓓ
5. Ⓐ Ⓑ Ⓒ Ⓓ
6. Ⓐ Ⓑ Ⓒ Ⓓ
7. Ⓐ Ⓑ Ⓒ Ⓓ
8. Ⓐ Ⓑ Ⓒ Ⓓ
9. Ⓐ Ⓑ Ⓒ Ⓓ
10. Ⓐ Ⓑ Ⓒ Ⓓ

11. Ⓐ Ⓑ Ⓒ Ⓓ
12. Ⓐ Ⓑ Ⓒ Ⓓ
13. Ⓐ Ⓑ Ⓒ Ⓓ
14. Ⓐ Ⓑ Ⓒ Ⓓ
15. Ⓐ Ⓑ Ⓒ Ⓓ
16. Ⓐ Ⓑ Ⓒ Ⓓ
17. Ⓐ Ⓑ Ⓒ Ⓓ
18. Ⓐ Ⓑ Ⓒ Ⓓ
19. Ⓐ Ⓑ Ⓒ Ⓓ
20. Ⓐ Ⓑ Ⓒ Ⓓ

21. Ⓐ Ⓑ Ⓒ Ⓓ
22. Ⓐ Ⓑ Ⓒ Ⓓ
23. Ⓐ Ⓑ Ⓒ Ⓓ
24. Ⓐ Ⓑ Ⓒ Ⓓ
25. Ⓐ Ⓑ Ⓒ Ⓓ
26. Ⓐ Ⓑ Ⓒ Ⓓ
27. Ⓐ Ⓑ Ⓒ Ⓓ
28. Ⓐ Ⓑ Ⓒ Ⓓ
29. Ⓐ Ⓑ Ⓒ Ⓓ
30. Ⓐ Ⓑ Ⓒ Ⓓ

POSTAL EXAM 473/473c
ANSWER SHEET

PRACTICE TEST 5: CODING AND MEMORY

Section 1: Coding

1. Ⓐ Ⓑ Ⓒ Ⓓ	13. Ⓐ Ⓑ Ⓒ Ⓓ	25. Ⓐ Ⓑ Ⓒ Ⓓ
2. Ⓐ Ⓑ Ⓒ Ⓓ	14. Ⓐ Ⓑ Ⓒ Ⓓ	26. Ⓐ Ⓑ Ⓒ Ⓓ
3. Ⓐ Ⓑ Ⓒ Ⓓ	15. Ⓐ Ⓑ Ⓒ Ⓓ	27. Ⓐ Ⓑ Ⓒ Ⓓ
4. Ⓐ Ⓑ Ⓒ Ⓓ	16. Ⓐ Ⓑ Ⓒ Ⓓ	28. Ⓐ Ⓑ Ⓒ Ⓓ
5. Ⓐ Ⓑ Ⓒ Ⓓ	17. Ⓐ Ⓑ Ⓒ Ⓓ	29. Ⓐ Ⓑ Ⓒ Ⓓ
6. Ⓐ Ⓑ Ⓒ Ⓓ	18. Ⓐ Ⓑ Ⓒ Ⓓ	30. Ⓐ Ⓑ Ⓒ Ⓓ
7. Ⓐ Ⓑ Ⓒ Ⓓ	19. Ⓐ Ⓑ Ⓒ Ⓓ	31. Ⓐ Ⓑ Ⓒ Ⓓ
8. Ⓐ Ⓑ Ⓒ Ⓓ	20. Ⓐ Ⓑ Ⓒ Ⓓ	32. Ⓐ Ⓑ Ⓒ Ⓓ
9. Ⓐ Ⓑ Ⓒ Ⓓ	21. Ⓐ Ⓑ Ⓒ Ⓓ	33. Ⓐ Ⓑ Ⓒ Ⓓ
10. Ⓐ Ⓑ Ⓒ Ⓓ	22. Ⓐ Ⓑ Ⓒ Ⓓ	34. Ⓐ Ⓑ Ⓒ Ⓓ
11. Ⓐ Ⓑ Ⓒ Ⓓ	23. Ⓐ Ⓑ Ⓒ Ⓓ	35. Ⓐ Ⓑ Ⓒ Ⓓ
12. Ⓐ Ⓑ Ⓒ Ⓓ	24. Ⓐ Ⓑ Ⓒ Ⓓ	36. Ⓐ Ⓑ Ⓒ Ⓓ

POSTAL EXAM 473/473c
ANSWER SHEET

Section 2: Memory

1. Ⓐ Ⓑ Ⓒ Ⓓ
2. Ⓐ Ⓑ Ⓒ Ⓓ
3. Ⓐ Ⓑ Ⓒ Ⓓ
4. Ⓐ Ⓑ Ⓒ Ⓓ
5. Ⓐ Ⓑ Ⓒ Ⓓ
6. Ⓐ Ⓑ Ⓒ Ⓓ
7. Ⓐ Ⓑ Ⓒ Ⓓ
8. Ⓐ Ⓑ Ⓒ Ⓓ
9. Ⓐ Ⓑ Ⓒ Ⓓ
10. Ⓐ Ⓑ Ⓒ Ⓓ
11. Ⓐ Ⓑ Ⓒ Ⓓ
12. Ⓐ Ⓑ Ⓒ Ⓓ

13. Ⓐ Ⓑ Ⓒ Ⓓ
14. Ⓐ Ⓑ Ⓒ Ⓓ
15. Ⓐ Ⓑ Ⓒ Ⓓ
16. Ⓐ Ⓑ Ⓒ Ⓓ
17. Ⓐ Ⓑ Ⓒ Ⓓ
18. Ⓐ Ⓑ Ⓒ Ⓓ
19. Ⓐ Ⓑ Ⓒ Ⓓ
20. Ⓐ Ⓑ Ⓒ Ⓓ
21. Ⓐ Ⓑ Ⓒ Ⓓ
22. Ⓐ Ⓑ Ⓒ Ⓓ
23. Ⓐ Ⓑ Ⓒ Ⓓ
24. Ⓐ Ⓑ Ⓒ Ⓓ

25. Ⓐ Ⓑ Ⓒ Ⓓ
26. Ⓐ Ⓑ Ⓒ Ⓓ
27. Ⓐ Ⓑ Ⓒ Ⓓ
28. Ⓐ Ⓑ Ⓒ Ⓓ
29. Ⓐ Ⓑ Ⓒ Ⓓ
30. Ⓐ Ⓑ Ⓒ Ⓓ
31. Ⓐ Ⓑ Ⓒ Ⓓ
32. Ⓐ Ⓑ Ⓒ Ⓓ
33. Ⓐ Ⓑ Ⓒ Ⓓ
34. Ⓐ Ⓑ Ⓒ Ⓓ
35. Ⓐ Ⓑ Ⓒ Ⓓ
36. Ⓐ Ⓑ Ⓒ Ⓓ

POSTAL EXAM 473/473c
ANSWER SHEET

PRACTICE TEST 6: ADDRESS CHECKING

1. Ⓐ Ⓑ Ⓒ Ⓓ
2. Ⓐ Ⓑ Ⓒ Ⓓ
3. Ⓐ Ⓑ Ⓒ Ⓓ
4. Ⓐ Ⓑ Ⓒ Ⓓ
5. Ⓐ Ⓑ Ⓒ Ⓓ
6. Ⓐ Ⓑ Ⓒ Ⓓ
7. Ⓐ Ⓑ Ⓒ Ⓓ
8. Ⓐ Ⓑ Ⓒ Ⓓ
9. Ⓐ Ⓑ Ⓒ Ⓓ
10. Ⓐ Ⓑ Ⓒ Ⓓ
11. Ⓐ Ⓑ Ⓒ Ⓓ
12. Ⓐ Ⓑ Ⓒ Ⓓ
13. Ⓐ Ⓑ Ⓒ Ⓓ
14. Ⓐ Ⓑ Ⓒ Ⓓ
15. Ⓐ Ⓑ Ⓒ Ⓓ
16. Ⓐ Ⓑ Ⓒ Ⓓ
17. Ⓐ Ⓑ Ⓒ Ⓓ
18. Ⓐ Ⓑ Ⓒ Ⓓ
19. Ⓐ Ⓑ Ⓒ Ⓓ
20. Ⓐ Ⓑ Ⓒ Ⓓ

21. Ⓐ Ⓑ Ⓒ Ⓓ
22. Ⓐ Ⓑ Ⓒ Ⓓ
23. Ⓐ Ⓑ Ⓒ Ⓓ
24. Ⓐ Ⓑ Ⓒ Ⓓ
25. Ⓐ Ⓑ Ⓒ Ⓓ
26. Ⓐ Ⓑ Ⓒ Ⓓ
27. Ⓐ Ⓑ Ⓒ Ⓓ
28. Ⓐ Ⓑ Ⓒ Ⓓ
29. Ⓐ Ⓑ Ⓒ Ⓓ
30. Ⓐ Ⓑ Ⓒ Ⓓ
31. Ⓐ Ⓑ Ⓒ Ⓓ
32. Ⓐ Ⓑ Ⓒ Ⓓ
33. Ⓐ Ⓑ Ⓒ Ⓓ
34. Ⓐ Ⓑ Ⓒ Ⓓ
35. Ⓐ Ⓑ Ⓒ Ⓓ
36. Ⓐ Ⓑ Ⓒ Ⓓ
37. Ⓐ Ⓑ Ⓒ Ⓓ
38. Ⓐ Ⓑ Ⓒ Ⓓ
39. Ⓐ Ⓑ Ⓒ Ⓓ
40. Ⓐ Ⓑ Ⓒ Ⓓ

41. Ⓐ Ⓑ Ⓒ Ⓓ
42. Ⓐ Ⓑ Ⓒ Ⓓ
43. Ⓐ Ⓑ Ⓒ Ⓓ
44. Ⓐ Ⓑ Ⓒ Ⓓ
45. Ⓐ Ⓑ Ⓒ Ⓓ
46. Ⓐ Ⓑ Ⓒ Ⓓ
47. Ⓐ Ⓑ Ⓒ Ⓓ
48. Ⓐ Ⓑ Ⓒ Ⓓ
49. Ⓐ Ⓑ Ⓒ Ⓓ
50. Ⓐ Ⓑ Ⓒ Ⓓ
51. Ⓐ Ⓑ Ⓒ Ⓓ
52. Ⓐ Ⓑ Ⓒ Ⓓ
53. Ⓐ Ⓑ Ⓒ Ⓓ
54. Ⓐ Ⓑ Ⓒ Ⓓ
55. Ⓐ Ⓑ Ⓒ Ⓓ
56. Ⓐ Ⓑ Ⓒ Ⓓ
57. Ⓐ Ⓑ Ⓒ Ⓓ
58. Ⓐ Ⓑ Ⓒ Ⓓ
59. Ⓐ Ⓑ Ⓒ Ⓓ
60. Ⓐ Ⓑ Ⓒ Ⓓ

POSTAL EXAM 473/473c
ANSWER SHEET

PRACTICE TEST 6: FORMS COMPLETION

1. Ⓐ Ⓑ Ⓒ Ⓓ
2. Ⓐ Ⓑ Ⓒ Ⓓ
3. Ⓐ Ⓑ Ⓒ Ⓓ
4. Ⓐ Ⓑ Ⓒ Ⓓ
5. Ⓐ Ⓑ Ⓒ Ⓓ
6. Ⓐ Ⓑ Ⓒ Ⓓ
7. Ⓐ Ⓑ Ⓒ Ⓓ
8. Ⓐ Ⓑ Ⓒ Ⓓ
9. Ⓐ Ⓑ Ⓒ Ⓓ
10. Ⓐ Ⓑ Ⓒ Ⓓ

11. Ⓐ Ⓑ Ⓒ Ⓓ
12. Ⓐ Ⓑ Ⓒ Ⓓ
13. Ⓐ Ⓑ Ⓒ Ⓓ
14. Ⓐ Ⓑ Ⓒ Ⓓ
15. Ⓐ Ⓑ Ⓒ Ⓓ
16. Ⓐ Ⓑ Ⓒ Ⓓ
17. Ⓐ Ⓑ Ⓒ Ⓓ
18. Ⓐ Ⓑ Ⓒ Ⓓ
19. Ⓐ Ⓑ Ⓒ Ⓓ
20. Ⓐ Ⓑ Ⓒ Ⓓ

21. Ⓐ Ⓑ Ⓒ Ⓓ
22. Ⓐ Ⓑ Ⓒ Ⓓ
23. Ⓐ Ⓑ Ⓒ Ⓓ
24. Ⓐ Ⓑ Ⓒ Ⓓ
25. Ⓐ Ⓑ Ⓒ Ⓓ
26. Ⓐ Ⓑ Ⓒ Ⓓ
27. Ⓐ Ⓑ Ⓒ Ⓓ
28. Ⓐ Ⓑ Ⓒ Ⓓ
29. Ⓐ Ⓑ Ⓒ Ⓓ
30. Ⓐ Ⓑ Ⓒ Ⓓ

POSTAL EXAM 473/473c
ANSWER SHEET

PRACTICE TEST 6: CODING AND MEMORY

Section 1: Coding

1. Ⓐ Ⓑ Ⓒ Ⓓ
2. Ⓐ Ⓑ Ⓒ Ⓓ
3. Ⓐ Ⓑ Ⓒ Ⓓ
4. Ⓐ Ⓑ Ⓒ Ⓓ
5. Ⓐ Ⓑ Ⓒ Ⓓ
6. Ⓐ Ⓑ Ⓒ Ⓓ
7. Ⓐ Ⓑ Ⓒ Ⓓ
8. Ⓐ Ⓑ Ⓒ Ⓓ
9. Ⓐ Ⓑ Ⓒ Ⓓ
10. Ⓐ Ⓑ Ⓒ Ⓓ
11. Ⓐ Ⓑ Ⓒ Ⓓ
12. Ⓐ Ⓑ Ⓒ Ⓓ

13. Ⓐ Ⓑ Ⓒ Ⓓ
14. Ⓐ Ⓑ Ⓒ Ⓓ
15. Ⓐ Ⓑ Ⓒ Ⓓ
16. Ⓐ Ⓑ Ⓒ Ⓓ
17. Ⓐ Ⓑ Ⓒ Ⓓ
18. Ⓐ Ⓑ Ⓒ Ⓓ
19. Ⓐ Ⓑ Ⓒ Ⓓ
20. Ⓐ Ⓑ Ⓒ Ⓓ
21. Ⓐ Ⓑ Ⓒ Ⓓ
22. Ⓐ Ⓑ Ⓒ Ⓓ
23. Ⓐ Ⓑ Ⓒ Ⓓ
24. Ⓐ Ⓑ Ⓒ Ⓓ

25. Ⓐ Ⓑ Ⓒ Ⓓ
26. Ⓐ Ⓑ Ⓒ Ⓓ
27. Ⓐ Ⓑ Ⓒ Ⓓ
28. Ⓐ Ⓑ Ⓒ Ⓓ
29. Ⓐ Ⓑ Ⓒ Ⓓ
30. Ⓐ Ⓑ Ⓒ Ⓓ
31. Ⓐ Ⓑ Ⓒ Ⓓ
32. Ⓐ Ⓑ Ⓒ Ⓓ
33. Ⓐ Ⓑ Ⓒ Ⓓ
34. Ⓐ Ⓑ Ⓒ Ⓓ
35. Ⓐ Ⓑ Ⓒ Ⓓ
36. Ⓐ Ⓑ Ⓒ Ⓓ

POSTAL EXAM 473/473c
ANSWER SHEET

Section 2: Memory

1. Ⓐ Ⓑ Ⓒ Ⓓ   13. Ⓐ Ⓑ Ⓒ Ⓓ   25. Ⓐ Ⓑ Ⓒ Ⓓ

2. Ⓐ Ⓑ Ⓒ Ⓓ   14. Ⓐ Ⓑ Ⓒ Ⓓ   26. Ⓐ Ⓑ Ⓒ Ⓓ

3. Ⓐ Ⓑ Ⓒ Ⓓ   15. Ⓐ Ⓑ Ⓒ Ⓓ   27. Ⓐ Ⓑ Ⓒ Ⓓ

4. Ⓐ Ⓑ Ⓒ Ⓓ   16. Ⓐ Ⓑ Ⓒ Ⓓ   28. Ⓐ Ⓑ Ⓒ Ⓓ

5. Ⓐ Ⓑ Ⓒ Ⓓ   17. Ⓐ Ⓑ Ⓒ Ⓓ   29. Ⓐ Ⓑ Ⓒ Ⓓ

6. Ⓐ Ⓑ Ⓒ Ⓓ   18. Ⓐ Ⓑ Ⓒ Ⓓ   30. Ⓐ Ⓑ Ⓒ Ⓓ

7. Ⓐ Ⓑ Ⓒ Ⓓ   19. Ⓐ Ⓑ Ⓒ Ⓓ   31. Ⓐ Ⓑ Ⓒ Ⓓ

8. Ⓐ Ⓑ Ⓒ Ⓓ   20. Ⓐ Ⓑ Ⓒ Ⓓ   32. Ⓐ Ⓑ Ⓒ Ⓓ

9. Ⓐ Ⓑ Ⓒ Ⓓ   21. Ⓐ Ⓑ Ⓒ Ⓓ   33. Ⓐ Ⓑ Ⓒ Ⓓ

10. Ⓐ Ⓑ Ⓒ Ⓓ   22. Ⓐ Ⓑ Ⓒ Ⓓ   34. Ⓐ Ⓑ Ⓒ Ⓓ

11. Ⓐ Ⓑ Ⓒ Ⓓ   23. Ⓐ Ⓑ Ⓒ Ⓓ   35. Ⓐ Ⓑ Ⓒ Ⓓ

12. Ⓐ Ⓑ Ⓒ Ⓓ   24. Ⓐ Ⓑ Ⓒ Ⓓ   36. Ⓐ Ⓑ Ⓒ Ⓓ

Notes

Notes

Notes

Notes

Notes

Notes